Praise for

30 Days to James by Dr. Bill Curtis is outstanding! Your spiritual life will be so much richer by spending a month in this great book of the Bible. I urge you to read it, absorb it, and allow God to teach you the practical and powerful truth found in it. Spend 30 days in James and your life will never be the same! Thank you Dr. Bill Curtis for this excellent resource!

—Dr. Doug Munton
Senior Pastor, First Baptist Church, O'Fallon, IL
Author of *30 Days to Acts* and *7 Steps to Becoming a Healthy Christian Leader*

30 Days to James is an expositional, gospel-centered Bible study that is written by a scholar yet designed for the local church. Dr. Bill Curtis explores the book of James to reveal truth that can transform lives. This book is exactly what local churches need to put in the hands of their members!

—Dr. Dwayne Milioni
Senior Pastor, Open Door Baptist Church, Raleigh, NC
Co-Founder, The Pillar Church Planting Network

Each time I read the book of James, I'm struck by how many ways this epistle — probably the earliest New Testament book written — addresses the specifics of our lives in the 21st century. In *30 Days to James*, Dr. Bill Curtis captures the practicality of James and connects its rich spiritual themes to real life. I challenge you to read this book for 30 days; it'll change you for years to come!

—Dr. Stephen Rummage
Senior Pastor, Bell Shoals Baptist Church, Brandon, FL
Award-winning author of *Engaging Exposition* and *Planning your Preaching*

Dr. Bill Curtis' new book, *30 Days to James*, is a well-written, practical guide for our daily walk with God. Its explanation of the meaning of each passage is exegetically sound and gospel-centered, with clear illustrations from life to which we all can relate. The inclusions of specific action steps for each day's reading provide both the encouragement and the means for the reader to immediately apply the truths of God's Word to their lives. I recommend that you get this great new book!

—Dr. David Beck
Professor of New Testament,
Southeastern Baptist Theological Seminary

In his new work, *30 Days to James*, Dr. Bill Curtis guides his readers with the keen mind of a scholar and the warm heart of an experienced pastor. That combination of warmth and knowledge welcomes readers to understand the writings of Jesus' brother and to apply those teachings to their lives. Dr. Curtis uses excellent exegesis to guide us towards spiritual growth, reflection, and life-change. *30 Days to James* is a compelling and challenging journey you'll want to experience!

—Dr. Chet Roden
Professor of Old Testament, Liberty School of Divinity
Author, *30 Days to Genesis*

I am thrilled to recommend *30 Days to James*! In this devotional commentary, Dr. Bill Curtis has demonstrated that it is possible to grasp the message of James both devotionally and doctrinally. On page after page he illustrates how James' epistle strikes a perfect balance between both the how and why of the Christian faith. Each chapter takes you deep into the theology of the epistle and wide into the practical implications of that theology for every facet of Christian living. After immersing yourself in this volume for 30 days, you'll walk away with a profound understanding of how God's Word should shape your life. If you've been searching for a book that will help you to grasp both the content of James and the consequences of that content for your own spiritual journey, then look no further than *30 Days to James*.

—Dr. Mark Howell
Senior Pastor, First Baptist Church, Daytona, FL
Author, *Exalting Jesus in 1 & 2 Thessalonians*

Finally! A devotional that is exegetically sound, theologically robust, and practically relevant. In *30 Days to James,* pastor-theologian Dr. Bill Curtis has written a study that engages the biblical text while also engaging the reader with a conversational style that brings out the rich gems of truth that are contained in the book of James. If you are looking to live and leave a legacy for the glory of God, join Dr. Curtis on this exciting 30-day journey.

—Dr. Kevin King
Professor of Preaching, Liberty School of Divinity

Living the Christian life is not merely about focusing on the heavenly "pie in the sky when you die." It is about following God in the gritty, challenging, here and now. Following Christ is practical. That is why Dr. Bill Curtis' new book, *30 Days to James*, is so important. It takes you on a journey through some of the most practical pages of the New Testament, the book of James. In this book you will learn how to obey God in your everyday life. This 30-day experience will show you how God guides your steps right here and right now.

—Dr. Greg Faulls
Senior Pastor, Bellevue Baptist Church, Owensboro, KY
Author, *From Dust to Destiny*

30 DAYS TO
JAMES

30 Days to James

A Devotional Commentary

Bill Curtis

Seed Publishing Group, LLC
Timmonsville, South Carolina

30 Days to James: A Devotional Commentary

Published by:
Seed Publishing Group
2570 Double C Farm Ln
Timmonsville, SC 29161
seed-publishing-group.com

Edited by:
Bill Curtis, Ph.D.
Dwayne Milioni, Ph.D.

To order additional copies of this resource visit
www.seed-publishing-group.com.

Library of Congress Control Number: 2015915170

ISBN-13: 978-0-9968412-0-7

1 2 3 4 5 6 7 8 9 10

Printed in the United States of America

For Lyla,

The one who knows all of my dreams
and chases them with me!

Contents

Foreword

I became a Christ-follower my sophomore year of college. Before then, I had no real desire to read the Bible. Actually, I had no desire to read anything, except for baseball stats! I remember leaving for college my freshman year, and my mom said to me, "You need to take a Bible with you." When I asked why, she said, "You might read it one day."

By God's grace, that day eventually came. About a year and a half after Mom's suggestion (and her many prayers), one of my baseball teammates, Stephen, led me to Christ. Following Stephen's example, I purchased a massive study Bible, and began reading the Bible like a glutton at a Golden Coral buffet. I couldn't get enough of the Word. I belonged to three different Bible studies on campus. We even did one event called "Crave" (based on 1 Peter 2:1-3), where a group of us read through the whole Bible out loud in ten days.

Prior to college, I had a reading comprehension problem. I was actually being tutored in reading. But when I began following Jesus, God granted me grace in this area, and soon I began memorizing large passages of Scripture. What is more, I felt as if the Bible was dynamically changing me. I even wrote on the outside edges of my big study Bible, "It's alive!"

After sensing a call to ministry the next year, I decided to go to New Orleans Baptist Seminary so I could study expository preaching under Jim Shaddix. Because I didn't have any prior religion courses, everything was new to me. I didn't know the seminary vocabulary. One of the courses I took immediately was called Hermeneutics. I didn't know what it meant (it sounded like the name of a Latin American middle infielder to me!), but everyone said it was a fundamental course and that I should take it my first year of seminary. And I did. In that course, I learned a lot about interpreting the Bible responsibly. I would go on to take a bunch more classes, and read a whole lot of books. Books on biblical theology (studying the storyline and themes of the whole Bible) helped me tremendously to not just study the details of a particular text, but to also see where it fits within redemptive history. This made me love the Bible even more, because I began to see Jesus as the Hero of Scripture, and this discovery was exhilarating.

Despite all of these things, I know that one's affection for the word of Christ and the Christ of the word can cool. But I don't want that to happen in my life. The apostle Paul didn't want Timothy's passion to cool either. Paul told this young minister:

> *But as for you, continue in what you have learned and have firmly believed, knowing from whom you learned it and how from childhood you have been acquainted with the sacred writings, which are able to make you wise for salvation through faith in Christ Jesus. All Scripture is breathed out by God and profitable for teaching, for reproof, for correction, and for training in righteousness, that the man of God may be complete, equipped for every good work. (2 Tim 3:14-17, ESV)*

Paul charged Timothy to continue in the word; to continue in what he has learned and what he has believed. Every Christian – not just "ministers" – needs to heed this exhortation. And why should we bother with the Bible? Paul says that the Bible leads us to Jesus; God speaks to us from it; and God changes us from the inside out by it.

Paul himself even models this ongoing passion for the word, as the war-torn apostle gives some final instructions to Timothy: "When you come, bring the cloak that I left with Carpus at Troas, also the books, and above all the parchments" (2 Tim 4:13). After all that Paul had experienced in his life of service to Jesus, he still wanted the books and the parchments. What an example for us! Never stop trusting and treasuring the Scriptures.

In light of the need for constant biblical nourishment, I am thrilled to see these devotional commentaries written by pastor-theologians. I wholeheartedly recommend this 30-Day study on the book of James. New Christians, seasoned believers, and interested non-believers will all benefit from it. As you explore this powerful and practical book of the Bible, with Dr. Curtis as a trustworthy guide, I pray that you will not only understand the word better, but in the words of James, that you may become a "doer of the Word."

—Dr. Tony Merida

Preface

I wrote this book for me—and people like me.

Now, let me explain. I love God, and I love to read and study his book, the Bible. In fact, that's what I do for a living. I'm blessed to lead a wonderful church, and I'm also an adjunctive professor for two large, evangelical seminaries. What this means is that I'm constantly studying and teaching God's word.

And that's just it—studying for my mind is one thing; meditating with my heart is another. That is why I love devotional studies. They help remind me that I must be a faithful worshiper before I can be a faithful teacher.

That's why I've written this book. *30 Days to James* is the kind of devotional that I love to read—a devotional that unites solid teaching with practical application. It's designed to give you a devotion to read every day for a month, along with some valuable resources for meditation, application, and prayer.

Honestly, my days are as crazy as yours, so you can read each day's devotion in 15-20 minutes. The study, however, will stay with you all day long! You can purchase either a hard copy or an eBook, whichever works best for your busy life. Further, this book is written in such a way that anyone, from new believers to life-long saints, will grow in their spiritual journey.

So, what are you waiting for?

One more thing . . . This book is part of a larger series of books that is being developed by Seed Publishing Group; it is called *30 Days to the Bible.* Each year, several new books will be added to this series until all the books of the Bible have been covered. Renowned scholars and pastors from around the country will be writing books for this exciting, new series. So, if you like *30 Days to James*, keep your eyes open for the next books in the series: *30 Days to Genesis, 30 Days to Acts, 30 Days to the Parables, 30 Days to John*, and *30 Days to Colossians*!

Finally, Seed Publishing Group is an indie publisher committed to bringing great resources to both individual Christians and the local church (please visit them at www.seed-publishing-group.com). As part of that commitment, they are partners with The Pillar Network for church planting (www.thepillarnetwork.com). $1 from each sale of *30 Days to James* goes directly to church plants throughout North America. Thank you for purchasing *30 Days to James*, and thank you for investing in church planting!

–Bill Curtis, Ph.D.

James 1:1

James, a servant of God and of the Lord Jesus Christ. To the twelve tribes in the dispersion: Greetings.

Legacy. It's a word rich in imagery and impact. At its core, a legacy is something of value that is passed down from one person to another. Often, it is used to describe the gifting of material possessions, but it may also be used to describe the transference of intangibles. For instance, a mother may leave her children and grandchildren a legacy of love, and a father may leave his children and grandchildren a legacy of laughter. As you can see, legacies cannot be built over night; they take time, energy, and intentionality to develop. As a result, if you want to leave a legacy, you've got to learn how to live a legacy.

That is the purpose of the book of James. There are few books in the Bible more practical than this one. In fact, it reads like a New Testament version of Proverbs, only shorter. Scholars believe that James, the half-brother of Jesus, wrote the book. James initially rejected Jesus as the promised Messiah (Jn 7:5), but later he believed (1 Cor 15:7). James was the lead Elder (Pastor) at the Church in Jerusalem. As you might imagine, the early church in Jerusalem was comprised primarily of Jewish Christians. In fact, the Greek word translated "assembly" that James uses to describe the church in 2:2

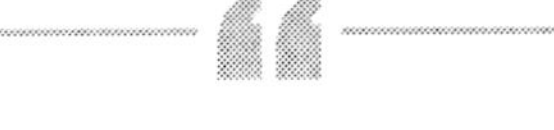

A legacy is something of value that is passed down from one person to another.

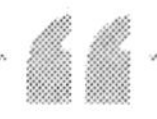

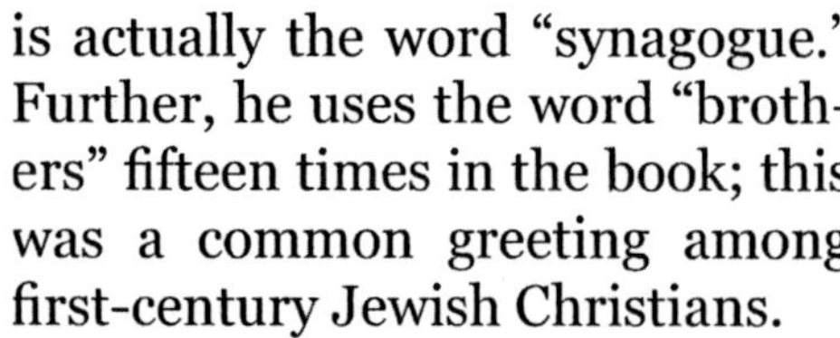

Authentic faith always reveals itself through godly lifestyle choices. Anyone can claim to be a Christian—only spiritual fruit reveals if someone is actually connected to Christ.

is actually the word "synagogue." Further, he uses the word "brothers" fifteen times in the book; this was a common greeting among first-century Jewish Christians.

James played an important role in the life of the early church, specifically during the meeting of the first church council, hosted in Jerusalem and recorded for us in Acts 15. As this chapter recounts, the Jerusalem Elders, the resident apostles, and Paul and Barnabas met to discuss the impact of the gospel upon Jewish and Gentile Christians. The amazing truth of the gospel is that both Jews and Gentiles can experience God's forgiveness and salvation by grace, through faith, apart from works. This was easier for Gentiles to accept than Jews, because the Gentiles had no previous understanding of the Old Testament law and sacrificial system. While people in the Old Testament had always been saved on the basis of faith (Rom 4), many in Israel had come to believe that salvation was a by-product of keeping the law (or attempting to, anyways). Consequently, many Jewish believers taught that while salvation was by faith, it should be accompanied by certain ceremonial observances like circumcision (Gal 2:15-3:29). James played a major role in this first church council, and he enunciated the council's conclusions, challenging Gentile believers to embrace certain Mosaic principles that would define their allegiance to Christ and their abhorrence of idolatrous worship practices (Acts 15:12-21).

James wrote his book to Jewish believers who were mentors of his church, many of whom had fled Jerusalem for various regions within the Roman Empire (i.e., "the dispersion"). Scholars believe that this occurred during the persecution that erupted during the reign of Herod the King, which resulted in the death of James (the brother of John), the imprisonment of Peter, and the persecution of Jewish Christians in general (Acts 12). Because the letter doesn't mention the first church council, it is safe to assume that James wrote this book between AD 44-49, which makes it the earliest book written in the New Testament.

James' ultimate goal is to equip us to live a legacy for the glory of God.

James' book is incredibly practical in nature. He challenged his readers, as he will challenge us, to understand the proper relationship between faith and works. As a Jewish believer, he understood that authentic faith always reveals itself through godly lifestyle choices. Anyone can claim to be a Christian—only spiritual fruit reveals if someone is actually connected to Christ (Jn 15:1-11). As you read his book, you will observe that he uses many analogies from nature to help us understand this spiritual truth. His book will challenge us to grow spiritually in both our walk and our witness.

So, what is James' ultimate goal? I believe it is to equip us to live a legacy for the glory of God. There is nothing more valuable that we can give to our wives or husbands, children, grandchildren, friends, neighbors, or this world than a legacy of faith. After all, a faith that is lived is a faith that can be believed. Real faith is on display when we face the greatest trials of our lives with endurance and grace. Real faith is on display when we treat every person with respect, because they are image-bearers of God. Real faith is on display when we control our speech and use it to encourage the people around us. Real faith is on display when we trust God with our hopes and plans, even when they don't come to fruition. Real faith is on display when we trust God in our suffering. This is the kind of faith that leaves a legacy and has an impact

A faith that is lived is a faith that can be believed.

on the people around us. This is the purpose of James, and for the next 30 days, we're going to let God use this amazing book to grow our faith!

Food for Thought

Everyone has a legacy—the only question is whether it is good or bad. Think about the legacy you're living today. Is it the kind you want to leave to your family and friends? Are you proactively striving to live a legacy of faith, or have you succumbed to a life where daily survival is the goal? Over the next 30 days, God is going to challenge you to get serious about living the gospel in a way that pleases him and builds a legacy of faith. Are you willing to let God grow your faith?

Faith in Action

Today, make a plan for working through this book. Check your calendar, and select the time every day when you will spend some time with God. Consider purchasing a journal to record your thoughts and prayers during the next 30 days. Tell someone you know that you're planning to work through this book, and ask him or her to hold you accountable to finish the study. Plan to give them a weekly update on your progress and growth.

Prayer

Spend time talking with God today about your desire to live and leave a legacy of faith. Ask God to reveal the areas of your life that he wants to refine as you work through this book. Commit to God your intention to complete this study over the next 30 days.

James 1:2-3

Count it all joy, my brothers, when you meet trials of various kinds, for you know that the testing of your faith produces steadfastness.

Have you ever had one of those days when nothing seems to go right? You know the kind of day I'm talking about. You oversleep and have to run around like a wild person trying to get ready for work. You make it to your meeting 15 minutes late, and then have to endure everyone's judgmental glances as you slip into the room. Finally, when your boss asks for your input, you realize that in your haste to leave the house, you left all of the material for your meeting on your desk at home. And to top it off, your boss chews you out in front of all of your peers.

We've all had trying days just like this one. But we have to admit—there are trials, and then there are TRIALS! While the morning I described above is difficult to navigate, it can't compare to the big trials of life. I can still remember when the son of one of my best buddies was going through chemotherapy in an attempt to treat a rare, life-threatening adrenal deficiency. I've watched as family members have experienced the pain of divorce after years of marriage. And, I know what it's like to get a phone call in the middle of the night and hear that your Dad has just died of a heart attack. These are the biggest trials we ever encounter in our lives.

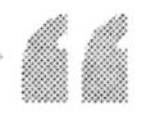

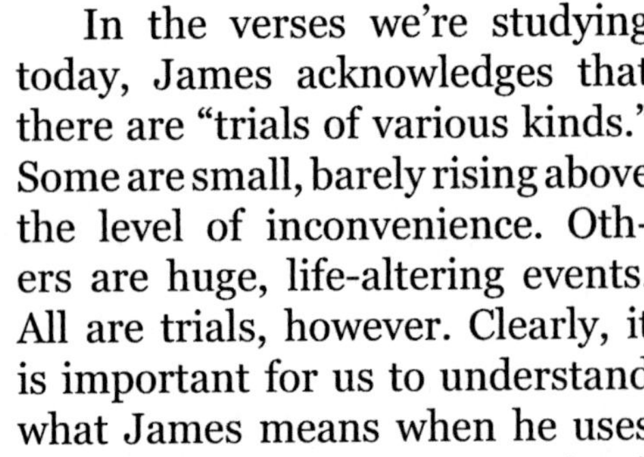

In the verses we're studying today, James acknowledges that there are "trials of various kinds." Some are small, barely rising above the level of inconvenience. Others are huge, life-altering events. All are trials, however. Clearly, it is important for us to understand what James means when he uses the word "trial." Literally, the word means "temptation." Interestingly, we determine how to translate it based upon who is doing the action. If Satan is the originator of the action, we translate it temptation, because his goal is always to trap us under the power of sin and its consequences. But if God is the originator of the action, we translate it trial, because his goal is the strengthening of our faith. So we can say it like this: when God is the source of a trial, it is always designed to improve us; God never intends for a trial to cause us to stumble.

When I read these verses I have one simple question: "If God loves me, why does he let me experience any trials at all?" I imagine that you may have asked this question yourself on occasion. Fortunately, James provides us with the answer. He writes, "You know that the testing of your faith produces steadfastness." There are two key concepts that we need to understand from this statement. First, we must understand what he means by the testing of our faith. The word translated "testing" refers to something with which we are all familiar. It refers to any type of exam designed to test someone's knowledge. Do you remember all of those tests you've taken in school? They were designed to see how much information you had actually learned about a subject. When we think about the trials God brings into our lives, it's best to think of them as similar kinds of exams.

But what is the purpose of God's exams? This brings us to the second key concept we must understand from this text. James tells us that God's exams are designed to assess the growth of our faith. The word translated "faith" in this verse is a very important word in the New Testament. It appears in numerous places, and it means belief in the divine truths of God, faith begins at the moment we accept Jesus Christ as our Savior and Lord. It continues as we live with confidence in the plan and promises of God.

Believe it or not, God is watching our lives for evidence of faith. He wants us to trust him in every circumstance that we encounter in life. When our boss chastises us in front of our peers, God is watching to see if we will be captured by anger or grace. When we hear that a family member has died suddenly, God is watching to see if we will rebel against his sovereignty or bow our hearts in surrender to his will. Every trial is a test of our faith in the plan and promises of God.

As we read the Bible, we encounter lots of people who are just like us—trying to trust and serve God in a fallen world. One of those men was Job. God tested Job to see how he would respond to the loss of his family, possessions, and health. Job trusted God, but he struggled to understand why God had allowed such massive heartache into his life. Ultimately, like Job, we may be tempted to ask the question "why," regardless of the strength of our faith. Thankfully, James provides us with the answer. He writes, "The testing of your faith produces steadfastness." The word translated "steadfastness" may be best understood as the word "endurance." We might literally describe steadfastness as "endurance under trial." In other words, it means that God's exams provide us with an opportunity to respond to adversity in a way that demonstrates faith in him.

> *If we never experienced adversity, when would we ever learn to trust God?*

Of course, we all struggle at times to grasp the necessity of faith and the trials that help produce it. I think it can be helpful to think about faith in relation to our everyday life. Faith is like a human muscle—it must be exercised to grow. All of us know what a challenge it is to grow our muscles. It takes commitment and effort. Our faith operates like a human muscle. When God brings a trial into our lives to test us, it provides us with the opportunity to exercise our faith. We trust God, and we see him work in our lives. When this happens, our faith grows stronger. Think about it, if we never experienced adversity, when would we ever learn to trust God? So God brings his exams into our lives to both test and strengthen our faith. The more we exercise our faith, the stronger our faith will become.

Because this faith-building process is essential for us, and because it reflects the goodness of a loving God, James encourages us to respond to trials with joy. He writes, "Count it all joy, my brothers, when you meet trials of various kinds, for you know that the testing of your faith produces steadfastness." If you're like me, you may wish that you could discuss this statement with James. "Count it all joy? Really? Are you kidding me? How in the world can I feel joy when I've lost a friend, or a job, or a house, or a spouse, or a child? How in the world can I face those types of trials with joy?"

I think it's a fair question to ask. I may be able to find joy when I'm late for work, but am I really supposed to feel joy if I lose my job? The answer to that question is "YES!" The word "joy" can mean, "rejoice," "celebration," and "gladness of heart," and it is used in numerous places throughout the New Testament. It is important to understand that joy is not the same thing as happiness. Happiness is based on the emotion we feel when we are confronted with good circumstances. Joy, on the other hand, is the state of being we experience when we walk with God by faith, even when we find ourselves facing one of God's tests.

Today, as we strive to pass our own customized exams, Jesus remains our greatest source of encouragement. When he was faced with the trial of the cross, the most significant moment in redemptive history, he responded with obedience, faith, and joy (Heb 12:1-2).

Food for Thought

Spend some time reflecting on some of the trials that God has allowed to come into your life. What was your response? Do you find yourself resisting God's purpose when he tests you or embracing his tests as gifts of grace? Are you facing a trial right now? Are you walking through it by faith or fear? Have you prayed and asked God to use the trial to build your faith and to allow your life to point others towards Jesus?

Faith in Action

Odds are you may face some trails today. Some will be the simple stuff of life; others, however, may test your faith. If God brings a significant trial into your life today, remember that he always has a divine purpose for it in your life and the lives of others. Consider how you can respond with a faith and joy that brings glory to God and reveals Jesus to others.

Prayer

In your prayer time today, talk with God about the trials you may be facing. Rather than asking God "Why?" (he may not ever tell you), ask instead for the wisdom to walk by faith throughout the trial. Ask God for strength and endurance, and ask him to help you live in a way that will open opportunities for sharing the gospel with others.

James 1:4

And let steadfastness have its full effect, that you may be perfect and complete, lacking nothing.

It is incredibly difficult to build endurance. Every time I watch world-class athletes compete, I'm amazed by their strength and conditioning. This is especially true of Olympic athletes, and one of my favorite Olympians is Michael Phelps. His swimming record in the Olympics is simply incredible. In the 2004 Olympics in Athens, he won six gold medals. In the 2008 Olympics in Beijing he did the unthinkable—he won gold medals in all eight individual and medley events in which he swam; a feat that no one had previously accomplished! Then, in the 2012 Olympics in London, he added four more gold medals, bringing his Olympic gold medal count to 18. And, when added with his four silver medals, his total Olympic medal count is an astounding 22, making him the most decorated Olympian in history! Clearly, Michael Phelps is a talented swimmer. If we're not careful, however, we'll assume that natural ability alone is responsible for the success of world-class athletes. Not so for Michael Phelps. In the years leading up to the Olympics, he maintained an unbelievable training routine. He was successful in the Olympics because he had spent time building the endurance necessary to compete in multiple races.

As we discovered in yesterday's study, God gives us tests so that we can exercise our spiritual faith muscles and build our spiritual endurance. Every test provides us with

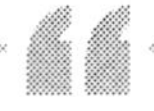

God wants to build our spiritual endurance, but we must cooperate with him for it to happen.

an indicator of our spiritual progress in the development of faith. In today's verse, James is going to challenge us to understand our role in this faith-building process: God wants to build our spiritual endurance, but we must cooperate with him for it to happen.

Verse four begins with a very simple word—"let." This word means "allow." It's a word that demonstrates that we are active participants in the working out of God's will in our lives. While God is the one doing the work, we must make choices about how we will respond to it. When James uses the tiny word "let" in this verse, he is telling us to cooperate with God!

Like many of you, I played competitive sports during my youth. While I loved the thrill of playing basketball games, practice was just plain death! There was no opposing team, no cheerleaders, and no crowds—just the sound of pounding feet and a coach's whistle echoing throughout an empty gym. But our coach understood something very important. The key to greatness isn't the ability to run the plays; it's the physical endurance necessary to outwork your opponent until the final whistle blows. And that kind of endurance cannot be obtained during the game—it's earned in the silence of lonely gyms.

What's interesting to me is that I *chose* to be a part of a team that required that kind of sacrifice. No one *made* me participate. Instead, I cooperated with the demands of my coach, and my teams experienced success. That is exactly what James is challenging us to do. We can choose to fight God every step of the way on our spiritual journey, or we can choose to "let steadfastness have its full effect" in our lives. What James means by this is simple. God has a specific, spiritual purpose that he wants to accomplish in our lives as a result of every test he gives us. He wants us to be ready to endure any trial that appears in our lives, because every new trial builds a greater level of spiritual endurance.

So what is the long-term benefit from the "testing of our your faith [that] produces steadfastness?" James states that it accomplishes something transformational in our lives. It makes us "perfect and complete, lacking nothing." When I hear that I'm supposed to be perfect, I get very worried! However, when we read the word perfect here in verse 4, it does not mean "sinless perfection." That, of course, cannot be obtained in this life. Instead, what it means is "completeness." It means that our lives have a sense of "wholeness."

Before we accepted Jesus into our lives as our Savior and Lord, we were separated from God by our sin. Becoming "whole" as a person was an impossible goal. But when Jesus saved us, he changed all of that. Because the Holy Spirit indwells us, we have the potential to become spiritually complete. Consequently, we can develop into the man or woman of God that he has called us to be.

The end result of this process is that we "lack nothing." In other words, we do not have to be spiritually deficient in any way. So it works like this. God sends trials into our lives to provide us with an exam. The exam is designed to test the growth of our faith. After all, our response to the trial reveals whether we trust God or ourselves. The process of passing the test through faith builds our spiritual endurance. When spiritual endurance exists in our lives, we are equipped to experience success in the middle of any test. And, success demonstrates that we are becoming spiritually whole. When this is the case, we lack nothing that is necessary to walk by faith. God's wants our faith in him to be so complete that we can face any trial with endurance and joy! As we conclude today's devotion, I want to encourage you to think about some prac-

> *We can choose to fight God every step of the way on our spiritual journey, or we can choose to "let steadfastness have its full effect" in our lives.*

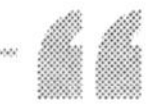

He wants us to read his word, seek the wisdom of wise counsel, and consider the witness of our lives to others.

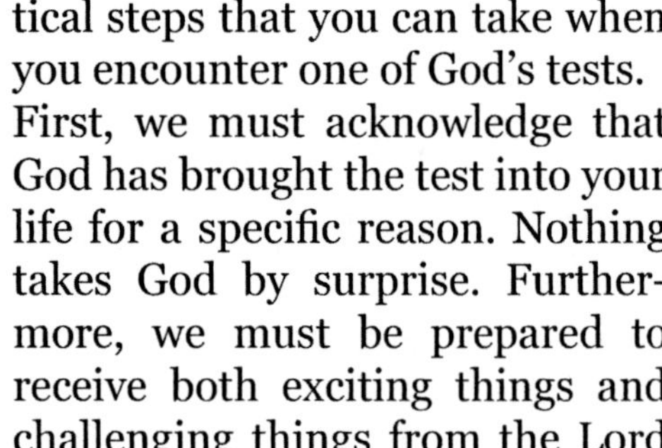

tical steps that you can take when you encounter one of God's tests. First, we must acknowledge that God has brought the test into your life for a specific reason. Nothing takes God by surprise. Furthermore, we must be prepared to receive both exciting things and challenging things from the Lord (Job 2:10). Finally, God intends to use every test for our good and the good of his kingdom (Rom 8:28). As a result, we must accept every trial as a divine act of God in our lives.

Second, we must choose to cooperate with God during the test. As we noted earlier, we can choose to fight God or work with him. We must "let steadfastness have its full effect." We must walk through the trial with our eyes turned towards heaven, looking for all of the ways that God wants to use our lives to impact others for the sake of the gospel.

Third, we must fight our fears through faith. When trials come, they often create a tremendous amount of fear in our lives. Fear is the enemy of faith. In fact, God says he is never the source of fear in our lives (2 Tim 1:7). When we're afraid, it is evidence of the fact that we are trusting in ourselves. That, in turn, will cause us to search for our own solutions to the trial we are facing. And, when we try to fix things ourselves, we generally make poor decisions. Instead, God wants us to trust him. He wants us to read his word, seek the wisdom of wise counsel, and consider the witness of our lives to others. Ultimately, he wants us to believe that the same God who has answered our prayers and supplied our needs in the past is fully capable to do the same thing in our present—even when we're facing the adversity of a trial.

Finally, God wants us to rejoice in the reality that he is at work in our lives. God has revealed that he initiates and completes the good work that he is doing in our lives

(Phil 1:6). While we cooperate with God's work through our faith and endurance, God is the one working out his eternal will of decree in our lives. As a result, we can have the joy of knowing that we will accomplish God's purpose as we walk with him by faith.

Are you experiencing a trial today? Are you navigating that trial with faith, endurance, and joy? Or, have you allowed the trial to create a fear in your life that has you fighting with God and looking for answers in all of the wrong places? Let me encourage you today to "let steadfastness have its full effect, that you may be perfect and complete, lacking in nothing."

Food for Thought

When God sends trials into our lives, it's always for our good. Nevertheless, receiving them as good gifts is often a challenge. How do you respond when you face trials in your life? Do you cooperate with God or do you fight against him? Consider some past trials you've faced. Would you do anything different if you were facing it today?

Faith in Action

Are you facing a trial today? If so, you may be teetering between fear and faith. Remember, faith is the only thing that can defeat fear. If you're tempted to make a decision out of fear today, step back and ask this question: "What would faith do in this situation?"

Prayer

If you're facing a trial today, ask God to give you the ability to navigate it by faith and not fear. Ask God to help you trust him, even if you're not sure what to do. And ask him to give you endurance to follow him.

James 1:5

If any of you lacks wisdom, let him ask God, who gives generously to all without reproach, and it will be given him.

There are only two prayers that God promises to answer. The first is the sinner's prayer, in which one acknowledges faith in Jesus Christ as Savior and Lord, and as a result, seeks God's forgiveness for sin. This forgiveness, made possible through the atoning death and bodily resurrection of Jesus, is made available to sinners as a result of God's grace. Romans 10:13 states, "Everyone who calls on the name of the Lord will be saved (For more information about the gospel, please read L.I.F.E. at the end of this book)."

The second prayer that God promises to answer is the prayer mentioned in our verse today—the prayer for wisdom. Wisdom is defined in a variety of ways: skill in the affairs of life, practical wisdom, sound judgment, and good sense. Wisdom incorporates all of these understandings, and they demonstrate the many ways that wisdom may have a positive impact on our lives.

The Bible reveals four important truths about wisdom. First, it reveals the root of wisdom. Proverbs 9:10 states, "The fear of the LORD is the beginning of wisdom, and the knowledge of the Holy One is insight." Here, wisdom is seen as being rooted in a healthy sense of awe towards God. Wisdom is a by-product of a personal relationship with God. Because we fear God, we will desire and seek his wisdom.

Wisdom is a by-product of a personal relationship with God.

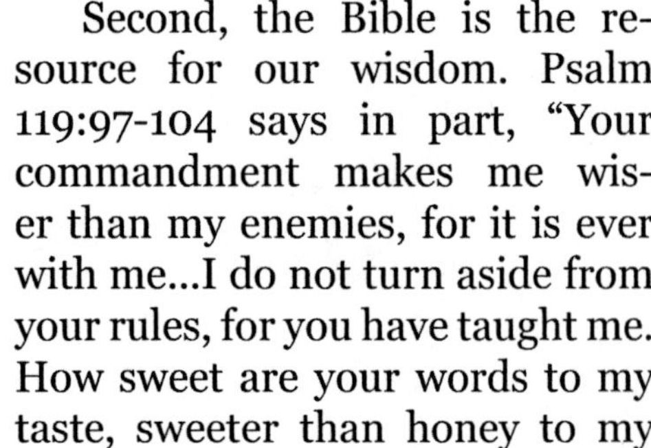

Second, the Bible is the resource for our wisdom. Psalm 119:97-104 says in part, "Your commandment makes me wiser than my enemies, for it is ever with me...I do not turn aside from your rules, for you have taught me. How sweet are your words to my taste, sweeter than honey to my mouth! Through your precepts I get understanding; therefore I hate every false way." Thankfully, God has given us the Bible so that we have access to his wisdom for our lives.

Third, the Bible reveals the requirement for obtaining wisdom in Proverbs 1:5, "Let the wise hear and increase in learning, and the one who understands obtain guidance." This verse emphasizes what may be the most important step in the process of obtaining wisdom—it is living with a teachable spirit. I've long believed that the common denominator behind all successful people is a willingness to be coached; to learn everything possible from a mentor in order to put it into practice in some area of their lives. In this verse we learn that God will make his wisdom known to everyone who will obtain and apply it.

Fourth, and finally, the Bible demonstrates the reward that accompanies God's wisdom. It has been said that "wisdom is its own reward," but God has even more in store for the wise man or woman. Proverbs 24:3-4 states, "By wisdom a house is built, and by understanding it is established; by knowledge the rooms are filled with all precious and pleasant riches." I love these verses! They remind us that "unless the LORD builds the house, those who build it labor in vain (Ps 127:1)." Similarly, they emphasize that wisdom not only helps build a life, but it also helps to establish it, like a house built on solid rock rather than sand (Mt 7:24-27). Finally, it teaches that wisdom applied leads to all types of blessings, both spiritual and tangible. These are the blessings of applying God's wisdom to our lives.

As we return to James 1:5, James reminds us of one final ingredient—prayer. He says, "If anyone lacks wisdom, let him ask God." Once we accept the truth of Scripture our final step is to ask God to apply his wisdom to our lives. The word translated in 1:5, "ask," has an interesting connotation. It was used to describe a child asking for something from a parent, or a beggar asking for help from a potential donor. It is a word that acknowledges the need of the one asking, and his or her complete inability to obtain the requested item apart from the generosity of another. Ultimately, we ask God for wisdom, because he is the only one who can grant it!

James next describes the way that God supplies wisdom to those who ask for it. First, God gives his wisdom "generously." This word literally means "bountifully." In other words, when we ask for wisdom, God doesn't give it to us in tiny doses—he pours it out all over us! Second, he gives us his wisdom "without reproach." In other words, God never criticizes us for lacking his wisdom. After all, he knows how desperately we need it, which explains why he has made provision for us to obtain it.

James concludes verse five with an amazing promise: "it will be given him" - five simple words that contain such amazing truth. God promises to give his wisdom to those who seek it and ask for it. God knows that apart from his wisdom we cannot apply his truth to our lives.

When we look at verse five in light of verses two and three, we discover some additional truth. Often, when we are experiencing one of God's trials in our lives, we may struggle to determine what God is doing and how we should respond. In this scenario, when we lack wisdom, God tells us to ask. While I may not receive an answer to "why" I'm going through a trial, I will always find the wisdom to know "how" to navigate the trial for God's glory and the good of his

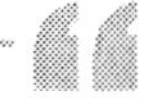

God will make his wisdom known to everyone who will obtain and apply it.

kingdom. Similarly, God's wisdom can reveal "what" to do while I'm in the trial. The pursuit of wisdom may help us in times of trial or when we need guidance for decisions in other areas of our lives, like our families or our finances.

Sadly, I can remember numerous times when I failed to seek God's wisdom when making important decisions. Early in our married life, when Lyla and I were expecting our daughter Cherie, we decided that we wanted a four-door sedan. We reasoned that it would make it easier to get her in and out of the car. So when it came to actually buying a car, however, I had little experience and even less wisdom. What followed was nothing short of a disaster. I found a car for sale in the classified ads and bought it. I knew nothing about the need to look at different makes and models, the questions to ask, or the dangers of buying a car from a stranger's back yard. Nevertheless, I drove a Subaru home and thought it was amazing! It was an automatic, had power locks and windows, and had the requisite four doors. It also had countless, unseen engine problems.

The first problem occurred in one of its maiden voyages. Some friends were riding with us to a Christian concert in Chattanooga when it cut off on the side of the interstate. Fortunately, I was able to reach one of my police buddies who carried us to the concert in the back of his patrol car! The second major issue developed on the way home from a trip to Florida. I'll never forget the hours spent in Valdosta, GA, trying to find a solution to a starter issue. For the rest of our 400 mile trip I had to start the car by placing a metal slug between the starter and a bolt on the engine mount. It was a disaster.

Finally, the car I paid $3,500 for wouldn't run at all. It just sat parked in front of my house, a painful reminder of my ignorance and incompetence. Exasperated, I found someone to buy it for $1,000. The final insult came when he poured in some transmission fluid, rocked the car back and forth a few times, and drove the car off like it was brand new. To this day, I've never recovered fully from that awful moment. Since then, God has taught me the principles that we've studied today, and I've learned that God does answer the prayer for wisdom, when we take the time to pray it!

So, what about you? When you're faced with a trial or a decision, do you ask God for wisdom, and go to the Scriptures to find it, or, do you try and work it out using your own ideas? I can assure you, God's plans are always best for every situation!

Food for Thought

What situation in your life requires wisdom right now? Is it related to a specific trial in your life? How are you trying to resolve the situation? Are you trying to solve the problem on your own or have you allowed God's Word to speak into the situation? If so, how?

Faith in Action

Sometimes we need the advice of godly, spiritual counselors when we're facing important decisions. Today, if you're tempted to make an important decision without God's wisdom, call a couple of strong Christian friends and ask their advice. God can use them to help you!

Prayer

This is an excellent day to begin asking God for wisdom. You will face circumstances today that require it! So, ask God to guide your steps as you make decisions today, and commit to let his word inform your choices.

James 1:6-8

But let him ask in faith, with no doubting, for the one who doubts is like a wave of the sea that is driven and tossed by the wind. For that person must not suppose that he will receive anything from the Lord. For that person must not suppose that he will receive anything from the Lord; he is double-minded man, unstable in all his ways.

I loved going places with my Dad when I was a kid. Often, Dad would stop at a drug store, and when he did, we would make our way to the candy counter. I would stare with wide eyes at rows of chocolate bars, licorice, suckers, and jaw breakers. Then, like a candy genie, Dad would say the words I loved to hear: "You can have one of anything you want!" Sadly, that is how many people view the gift of prayer. They envision God as a cosmic genie, ready to answer any prayer offered with enough faith. In fact, many people use our text for today as proof for this position.

The Scriptures reveal a very different picture of prayer, however. They reveal a God who is sovereign over all things, not one who succumbs to the selfish whims of finite people. Because God is infinite in knowledge and power, he knows the best outcome for every situation and established his will accordingly. Yet, he urges us to "cast our cares upon him, because he cares for us (1 Pt 5:7)." Ultimately, as Jesus himself acknowledged (Lk 22:42), God answers prayers that agree with his Sovereign plans (1 Jn 5:14-15). And this is where our text for today comes into focus.

> *Because God is infinite in knowledge and power, he knows the best outcome for every situation and wills accordingly.*

As we saw yesterday, God promises to answer the prayer for wisdom. As today's verses reveal, however, God says that there is one necessary ingredient in the prayer for wisdom—faith (v.6) The Greek word for faith means a confident trust in someone or something; it is belief revealed by action. Every time I strap into a giant roller coaster I'm demonstrating faith. I feel my body compressed by the force as the coaster races, banks, loops, and corkscrews. The only thing that keeps me from plunging to my death is the roll bar. I always give a sigh of relief when I finally arrive back at the loading area. Now, that's faith! The prayer for wisdom reveals the same thing about us. It demonstrates our confidence in God's promises.

As verse six continues, we see that doubt is the greatest enemy of faith. This word, sometimes translated "wavering," carries with it a slightly different meaning than our English word "doubt." More specifically, it means to oppose or contend with something. Consequently, the "doubt" referred to here is not the inability to believe that God can give wisdom. God has already provided us with all the wisdom we need in the Bible, to live for his glory (2 Pet 1:3). Rather, it is the internal struggle to believe that God's wisdom is best in every situation. It is the battle of wills that occurs when I encounter God's truth. Ultimately, when I choose to do things my own way on the basis of my own wisdom, I have chosen to oppose God's ways and God's wisdom.

The remainder of verse six provides the warning against this type of foolish decision, "The one who doubts is like a wave of the sea that is driven and tossed by the wind." There are few things in life more frightening to me than a storm on the water. When I was a boy, my Dad and I were caught out on a huge lake during a fast-approaching thunderstorm. Our tiny boat, with its small motor, could not outrace the storm, and soon we were at the mercy of the swirling, churning waves. By God's grace we escaped death that day, but I learned an invaluable lesson: wind-blown waves are dangerous and unpredictable.

This is the picture God uses to describe the condition of our lives when we doubt his wisdom. Rather than experiencing peace and safety, we are immediately at risk. The choices we make using our own "wisdom," and in contradiction to Scripture, place us in harms way. And the consequences of those poor choices may lead to catastrophe in our lives. There is a strong connection in Scripture between faith and obedience.

James continues with a warning: "For that person must not suppose that he will receive anything from the Lord." God promises to answer the prayer for wisdom. He provides the principles for that wisdom in his word. The prayer for wisdom is the prayer to properly understand and apply these biblical principles in our lives. However, if we ask God to grant us wisdom, but we doubt the truth of his word, the request will go unanswered by God. Our own lack of faith will stand in the way of the answer God has provided for us.

In verse eight, James provides a final description of the person who doubts God's wisdom, "He is a double-minded man, unstable in all his ways." There are two key words to understand in this verse. The first, translated "double-minded," refers to someone who has divided loyalties. It carries with it the concept that Elijah referenced when he challenged the people to choose whether to worship God or Baal. He asked them, "How long will you go limping between two opinions (1 Kgs 18:21)?" They couldn't decide whom they would worship, God or Baal. They were "double-minded." People who vacillate between their wisdom and God's wisdom do the

Wind-blown waves are dangerous and unpredictable.

People who doubt God's wisdom are always trying to find solid footing for their lives.

exact same thing. They can't make up their minds who to believe.

The second key word in this verse is translated "unstable." It means to be unsettled. In other words, the people who "limp between two opinions" consistently struggle in their decision-making.

Several years ago, I walked on to a construction site. Unknowingly, I walked into a room where the workers had spread a sealant on the floor. After three steps, I began to slip—it was like I was walking on ice. I could barely keep my balance, and it took all of my effort not to fall! Slowly, I inched my way back to the door. You can imagine my relief when I was back on "solid" ground. You've probably had a similar experience with unsettled footing in your own life. People who doubt God's wisdom are always trying to find solid footing for their lives.

God wants us to ask for wisdom, discover wisdom, and apply wisdom to our lives, yet we may struggle to learn how to do this. Here are some principles to guide us in this process. First, we must have a personal relationship with Jesus Christ. This relationship requires three things from us. First, we must recognize that God loves us and wants to have a relationship with us (Jn 3:16). As awesome as this sounds, we have a problem that stands in the way. That problem is sin. The Bible says that sin isolates us from God—it keeps us from having a personal relationship with him (Rom 3:23; 6:23). Second, God's love is so amazing, though, that he sent his one and only son Jesus to provide forgiveness for our sins through his death and resurrection (Rom 5:8; 1 Pet 2:21-25). Third, God has made forgiveness available, but it isn't automatic. We must make a personal decision to receive Jesus as our Savior and Lord (Rom 10:9-10). When we do this, we have the promise of forgiveness and the opportunity to enjoy God forever (Acts 16:31; Jn 14:1-6). We will never be willing to embrace God's wisdom if we don't embrace Christ first.

Second, we must acknowledge our need for God's wisdom. We will never seek God's wisdom until we believe that God's plans for us are always the best plans, and his guidelines for living are always the best guidelines. If we're not careful, we'll follow our own wisdom in the trouble-free seasons of our lives and only look for God's wisdom when things are tough. But this is the definition of the "double-minded" person, and we must avoid this at all cost. We need God's wisdom in every situation.

Third, we must study God's word diligently and apply it consistently. Many people want to apply God's wisdom, but they don't know how. There is only one solution to this problem— we must spend time in God's word! There are no shortcuts here. God will answer our prayer for wisdom and reveal it through his word. But he won't do the study for us. Wisdom is a reward for those who take the time to learn and apply God's word.

Fourth, we must seek godly counsel regularly. God's word teaches us that there is safety in a multitude of counselors (Pr 11:14). However, the counselor must be men and women of God who know the Bible. Seeking counsel from another "double-minded" person is of no benefit. When we are seeking to follow God's wisdom, input from godly counselors is a great help.

Fifth, we must pray for wisdom. That act of praying demonstrates our dependence upon God and our desire to make decisions that are pleasing to him. This positions us to receive all of the blessings that come from obedience to the wisdom of God. Remember, God promises to answer this prayer for us.

Sixth, and finally, we must trust God completely. This is the essence of faith. We must believe that God's word contains the truth that we need to make wise decisions, and that God will direct our steps as we apply it (Ps 37:23; Pr 3:5-6).

Food for Thought

The prayer for wisdom requires us to accept that God's truth is best in every situation. Have you grown in your faith to the place where you believe this? If not, what is holding you back? How does your faith need to grow, and what are some steps you can take to begin this process?

Faith in Action

Take an inventory of the six principles necessary to receive God's wisdom. How many of them are you currently practicing? If you're weak in some of these areas, brainstorm some ways to grow in these areas today.

Prayer

Spend time talking with God today about the depth of your faith and your challenges in trusting him. Be specific. Ask God to grow your faith as you trust in his character, word, and will.

James 1:9-11

Let the lowly brother boast in his exaltation, and the rich in his humiliation, because like a flower of the grass he will pass away. For the sun rises with its scorching heat and withers the grass; its flower falls, and its beauty perishes. So also will the rich man fade away in the midst of his pursuits.

Contentment may be the most challenging attitude to develop in all of life. Seemingly everywhere we look today we find examples of discontentment. Some people are discontent with politics, the economy, and culture. Others are discontent with their jobs, their spouses, their children, their stress levels, their weight, and their situation in life.

James has been instructing the church to find joy in the trials of life. As we've already seen, those trials produce steadfastness, and ultimately, spiritual maturity. In the middle of those trials, however, we need God's wisdom, which he promises to all those who ask for it with real faith—a faith that will strive to understand and obey God's truth. Then, almost randomly, we encounter the truth contained in verses 9-11. These verses teach us an important truth: Contentment is the tangible expression of faith. Honestly, these verses catch us off guard when we first read them. They feel out of context here. Yet, upon closer examination, we find that they serve as an illustration for the process of facing trials with biblical wisdom.

James was the pastor of the church in Jerusalem. This church suffered great hardship and persecution fol-

Contentment is the tangible expression of faith.

lowing the ascension of Jesus. Many Jewish Christians suffered economic hardships because of their faith. So much so that the apostle Paul raised money from the churches in Macedonia to help provide for their needs (2 Cor 8:9). It appears, then, that financial hardship was one of the specific trials they were facing.

When we read these verses, however, we notice that there was a group of believers in the church that was financially successful. We have no way of knowing how many believers fell into this category, but it was enough to create tension in the church among those who were struggling financially. James is providing wise counsel to his folks, regardless of their financial situation.

He begins be providing an admonition to those who were experiencing financial trials. He describes them as "lowly brothers." This phrase referred to those who because of humble circumstances were incapable of earning significant resources. Remember, these humble circumstances may have resulted from their status in society as a result of birthright or persecution. To these brothers, James challenges them to "boast in their exaltation." The word "boast" means to "glory, or celebrate." Specifically, James encourages them to celebrate their forever relationship with Jesus, which is unaffected by one's net worth.

Both Jesus and Paul reinforce what James is teaching in this text. When Jesus told the parable of the rich landowner who wanted to build new barns, he was teaching this principle: "Take guard against all covetousness, for one's life does not consist in the abundance of his possessions (Lk 12:13-21)." Similarly, Paul challenged the Romans to embrace suffering (including financial) by remembering this truth: "Through him we have also obtained access by faith into this grace in which we stand, and we rejoice in hope of the glory of God (Rom 5:1-5)." This hope is the hope of an eternity in the presence of God, not the health, wealth, and prosperity of this world. Our salvation is the most valuable possession we will ever have, and it is available to all—even the poorest person on earth.

Many times, when we look at the wealthy people around us, including those who reject the name of Jesus, we are tempted to covet their money and become discontent with our circumstances. But James reinforces the biblical truth that our lack of financial resources has no bearing on all of the heavenly blessings we have in Christ (Eph 1:3), including forgiveness, justification, adoption, sanctification, glorification, and all of the rewards and blessings of heaven.

In verses 10-11, James uses the word "rich" to refer to those people in the church who were financially successful. James challenges his rich folks to "boast, or celebrate," in their "humiliation." In Scripture, humility is a defining character trait of believers. Yet, humility is often difficult to define. In biblical terms, humility is the proper response of a finite, sinful person to an infinite, holy God. When we contemplate God in all of his glory and holiness, our only proper response is to acknowledge his greatness and our sinfulness. This is the essence of humility. It is acknowledging that we are totally dependent upon God for every gift of grace, including both our physical and spiritual blessings. The opposite of this attitude is pride. Pride attempts to convince us that we are responsible for our own blessings, including our financial resources.

James understood that personal possessions and financial security could become a significant source of pride in his wealthy people. It could tempt them to trust in themselves rather than God for their provision. As a result, he challenges them to "boast...in their humiliation." And, he provides them with a familiar object lesson to help them

"When we contemplate God in all of his glory and holiness, our only proper response is to acknowledge his greatness and our sinfulness."

> *Financial blessings are a gift of God's grace and are given for more than personal enjoyment. They carry with them a great responsibility and obligation for use in kingdom endeavors.*

walk in humility. James turns the attention of his readers to a spring meadow. The field is full of beautiful flowers awaking to the dawn of a new day. Soon, however, the sun rises with its scorching heat, and by midday, the flowers have faded, their beauty tarnished forever. James' meaning is clear: everything dies—even the rich and powerful.

With this as the backdrop, James challenges his wealthy members to view their finances with humility. Money does not have the power to either extend one's life or merit the approval of God. It is simply a tool to be used for God's glory as it is invested in God's kingdom. It does, however, have the potential to drag people away from God and his kingdom purposes.

Paul warned Timothy about this very real temptation. He writes, "Those who desire to be rich fall into temptation, into a snare, into many senseless and harmful desires that plunge people into ruin and destruction. For the love of money is a root of all kinds of evils. It is through this craving that some have wandered away from the faith and pierced themselves with many pangs (1 Tim 6:9-10)." When love for money transcends love for God, people make choices based upon greed rather than grace. This can only lead to heartache.

Instead, believers with significant financial resources should view their money with humility. Financial blessings are a gift of God's grace and are given for more than personal enjoyment. They carry with them a great responsibility and obligation for use in kingdom endeavors.

Which group in the Jerusalem church do you identify with today? Do you feel like the lowly brother in verse 9? If so, there are several things you can do. First, acknowledge that God is sovereign over everything in your life, even your money. Second, consider the possibility that your financial issues may be the result of poor stewardship at some level. If that's the case, there are great Christian resources available to help you learn to manage your money better. Third, begin to pray about opportunities to increase your resources. Perhaps you could consider seeking a new job or going back to school. This might increase your financial earning prospects. Fourth, pause to do a spiritual inventory. God's blessing, including in the area of one's finances, follows after those who live in obedience to him. Are you living for God's glory today? Are you faithfully using your spiritual gifts in his church? Are you honoring God by obediently giving your tithe through your local church? God blesses the obedient life, and God provides financial resources to those who are obedient stewards of them.

On the other hand, do you feel like the rich man in verse 10? When you think of your life, do you feel like God has blessed you in amazing ways financially? If so, there are some things God wants you to do as well. First, acknowledge that God is sovereign over your financial resources. Second, remember that your finances are a gift from God and must be used for the good of his kingdom. Third, begin to pray that God will make you more generous than you've ever been. The tithe is only the starting point for the child of God. If you've been blessed with wealth, you must look for opportunities to support kingdom endeavors. Ask God to give you a vision for church planting, foreign missions, and the needs of the poor. Fourth, pause to do a spiritual inventory. Greed is an enemy of the gospel. Do you struggle with a desire to hoard your money rather than invest in God's kingdom? Are you tempted to invest all of your money in things that will decay? Have you attempted to define for yourself how much is enough?

When love for money transcends love for God, people make choices based upon greed rather than grace. This can only lead to heartache.

Financially favored believers must view their finances as loans from God for kingdom projects.

Ultimately, James 1:9-11 is about finding contentment in regards to one's financial situation. Paul said, "I have learned in whatever situation I am to be content. I know how to be brought low, and I know how to abound. In any and every circumstance, I have learned the secret of facing plenty and hunger, abundance and need. I can do all things through him who strengthens me (Phil 4:11-13)." Contentment is not based upon circumstance—it is based upon faith. It requires trusting God to supply all of our needs, and then accepting that provision, whatever it may be, as a good gift from him. Today, embrace contentment in every area of your life, including your finances!

Food for Thought

When we think about money, our thoughts about contentment are often based more upon what others have than upon what we need. How do you measure your financial situation? Do you find yourself looking at the possessions of others with longing eyes? Do measure your financial success on the basis of the toys you can afford to buy? Do you see your financial surplus as personal resources or kingdom resources? The answer to these questions reveal much about your perspective on money and potential for contentment. Spend some time today thinking about a God-centered view of money and how you can make biblical stewardship the goal of your financial strategy.

Faith in Action

Conduct a personal contentment inventory of your life. What things in your life make you feel discontent? What is the source of your discontentment in those areas? What does your discontentment reveal about your relationship with God? Identify how James 1:9-11 and Philippians 4:9-13 can help you embrace contentment in those areas of your life.

Prayer

Today, talk with God about the areas of your life where you're struggling with contentment. This could include your finances, your job, your marriage, your possessions, or your perceived lack of opportunities in some area. Ask him to teach you how to trust him in these areas. Continue to ask for wisdom about how to deal with these situations, and ask him to help you be content as you live your life today!

James 1:12

Blessed is the man who remains steadfast under trial, for when he has stood the test he will receive the crown of life, which God has promised to those who love him.

For many Christians, contentment is an illusive dream. They know that it's God's will for them to be content, but there's always something standing in the way of actually achieving it. These are folks I call "If Only" believers. I hear their statements often: "If only my husband was more godly, I'd be content in my marriage." "If only my boss was more understanding, I'd be content with my job." "If only we had more money, I'd be content in my finances." "If only God would give me what I want, I'd be content in my faith." The examples go on, and on, and on.

James provides a different picture of contentment, however. He challenges us to live with contentment even in difficult situations, when we "face trials of various kinds." Anyone can feel content when the journey is easy; it's the detours of life that test the validity of our contentment. James teaches us that the testing of our faith produces endurance, and endurance is important for spiritual growth and maturity. He reminds us that God promises to give us all of the wisdom we need to practice contentment, even if we're struggling with feelings of inferiority because of our financial situation.

In today's text, however, we learn that God affirms those who live with contented hearts. James begins this verse with the word "blessed." When we hear that word, we tend to think about the word "happy." Clearly, happi-

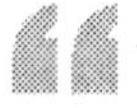

> *Anyone can feel content when the journey is easy; it's the detours of life that test the validity of our contentment.*

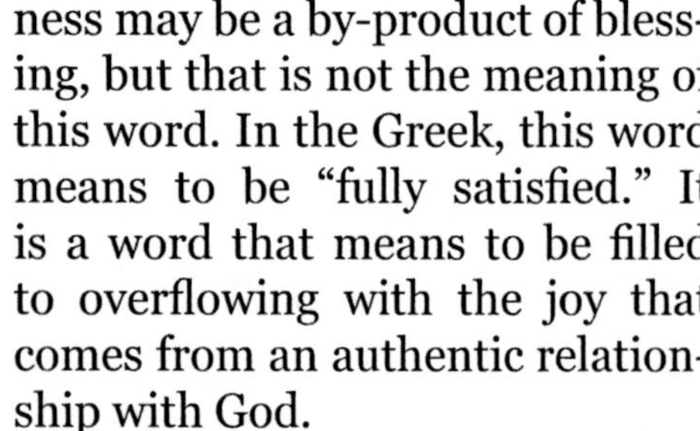

ness may be a by-product of blessing, but that is not the meaning of this word. In the Greek, this word means to be "fully satisfied." It is a word that means to be filled to overflowing with the joy that comes from an authentic relationship with God.

But James further clarifies how this joy is experienced. In 1:2, he told us to "count it all joy . . . when you meet trials of various kinds." While we tend to run from trials, God wants us to embrace them as gifts designed to build our spiritual endurance. Now, in 1:12, he continues this theme when he says that those who "remain steadfast under trial" will be fully satisfied with joy! The word translated "steadfast" here is the same word we found in 1:2. It means to "endure under adversity." Embracing trials by faith is challenging for us to do. It requires us to "stand the test." This phrase means to be "tried by fire." It's a phrase that was used to refer to the smelting process by which precious metals are refined. God uses trials to refine our faith. The refining process of trials break down our natural, sinful, selfishness and build up our supernatural, spiritual, faith in God.

If we respond poorly to God's trials, we are destined to face them over and over again until God's desired end is accomplished in us. But if we embrace them, we discover that God has great benefits in store for us. James tells us that when we endure trials by faith, we will receive the "crown of life, which God has promised to those who love him." The meaning of this phrase is difficult to interpret. Many scholars interpret this as the future promise of eternal life with God and its amazing rewards. We would be in error to suggest that James has no eschatological truth in mind when he uses these words. It is more likely, however, that James is referring primarily to the favor of God in this life when he uses this phrase. James' entire book is designed to help us understand that our practical, daily choices impact our spiritual journey. It is better to think of the phrase like this: "When we respond to God's trials with faith, we will experience the joy of God's favor in our daily lives."

It is interesting to note that James links this faith response to the premier motive of the heart—love. Jesus affirmed that the greatest commandment in the law is to "love the Lord your God with all your heart and with all your soul and with all your might (Dt 6:5)." James reminds us that God promises to reward obedience that results from an authentic love for him.

All of us want to experience the blessing and favor of God. While many of today's false teachers want you to believe that you can command the favor of God through "name it and claim it" practices, God reminds us that there is only one way to receive his favor—it is to live a life motivated by love, surrendered through obedience, and joyfully content in the middle of every circumstance.

This is a lofty goal! If you're like me, you may find that pursuing this as a lifestyle goal is challenging at best and discouraging at worst. I find that I struggle to love God with all of my heart, which leaves me susceptible to daily rebellion and disobedience, which in turn makes me vulnerable to responding to trials with fear rather than faith.

As I've grown in the Lord, however, I've discovered that embracing God's purposes, and the blessings they produce, requires me to embrace four fundamental truths about God and his will for my life. Understanding and embracing these truths has totally changed my perspective on the Christian life, and they can do the same for you!

> *"God reminds us that there is only one way to receive his favor—it is to live a life motivated by love, surrendered through obedience, and joyfully content in the middle of every circumstance."*

First, God is sovereign over the circumstances of our lives, both good and bad. When God allowed Satan to bring trials into Job's life, Job was suddenly im-

God is sovereign over the circumstances of our lives, both good and bad.

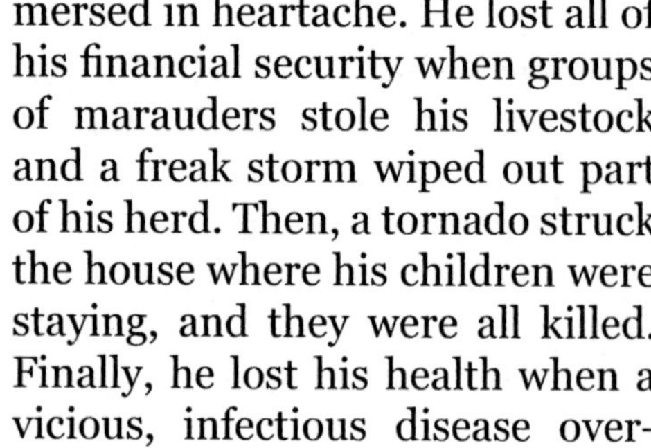

mersed in heartache. He lost all of his financial security when groups of marauders stole his livestock and a freak storm wiped out part of his herd. Then, a tornado struck the house where his children were staying, and they were all killed. Finally, he lost his health when a vicious, infectious disease overwhelmed his body.

I wonder how we would respond if this accumulation of events occurred in our own lives? Many, I fear, would turn their backs on God, blaming him for this difficult trial. Yet, James tells us to "count it all joy." How do we reconcile this? Job gives us the answer with his simple statement of faith: "Naked I came from my mother's womb, and naked shall I return. The LORD gave, and the LORD has taken away; blessed be the name of the LORD (Job 1:21)." This is one of the most beautiful statements about the sovereignty of God in the Bible. Job has just lost every significant, earthly thing in his life, but his life is fully surrendered to God regardless of his circumstances. Since God is the source of all of his blessings, it is his prerogative to take them back if it serves his purpose. Job understood that God is deserving of praise in both instances. He affirms this when he answers his wife's bitterness with these words, "Shall we receive good from God, and shall we not receive evil (Job 2:10)?"

This is the ultimate question for every believer. We are always excited to receive God's blessings. But when we face hardship, we are quick to question God and his purposes for our lives. In fact, many believers who fail to understand the significance of God's sovereign will for their lives often turn their backs on God after experiencing hardship. This sinful response leads them further from God and from his blessing.

Job's response, however, reveals that it is the proper one: "In all this Job did not sin or charge God with wrong

(Job 1:22)." Rather than being a source of fear, the sovereignty of God is our source of hope. We are not living lives of random chance. God has an eternal, kingdom purpose for us, and he works both his blessings and trials together for good in our lives (Rom 8:28).

Second, everything we possess is a gift of God's grace. If we're honest, we deserve nothing from God but judgment. Yet, he has chosen to shower us with grace because of his love. That grace has made our salvation possible, and with it, we have received "every spiritual blessing in the heavenly places (Eph 1:3)." Among these gifts is the promise of God's provision of our needs.

In the Sermon on the Mount, Jesus affirmed God's promise to meet our needs. He taught, "Do not be anxious, saying, 'What shall we eat?' or 'What shall we drink?' or 'What shall we wear?' For the Gentiles seek after these things, and your heavenly Father knows that you need them all. But seek first the kingdom of God and his righteousness, and all these things will be added to you (Mt 6:31-33)." God's faithful provision of our daily needs is a gift of grace. As a loving Father, however, God often blesses his children with the desires of their hearts. "Delight yourself in the LORD, and he will give you the desires of your heart (Ps 37:4)."

In Scripture, God is the acknowledged provider of both our needs and wants. But if we look carefully at these verses, we will note a very interesting principle: God supplies our needs and wants in proportion to our delight in him and his kingdom purposes. In Matthew, Jesus says that the pursuit of God's kingdom is the precursor to the meeting of our needs. In Psalms, David says that it is our delight in the LORD that leads to the granting of our heart's desires.

Our self worth is defined by who we are in Christ, not the things that we possess.

While God is the provider of these undeserved gifts of grace, he is also the originator of the trials that test our faith and build our

We will never experience true contentment until we understand that we have significance in life solely on the basis of our personal relationship with God.

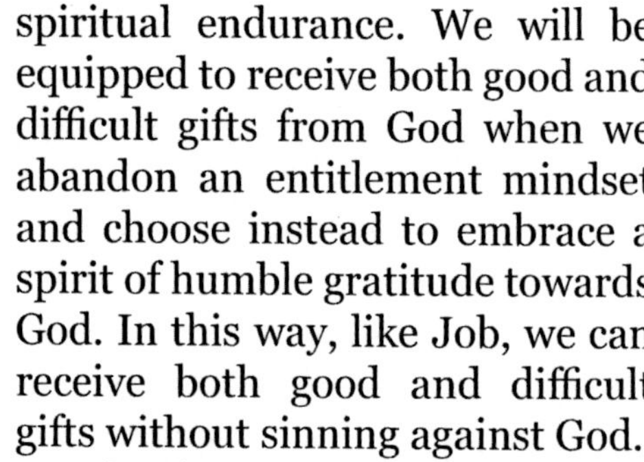

spiritual endurance. We will be equipped to receive both good and difficult gifts from God when we abandon an entitlement mindset and choose instead to embrace a spirit of humble gratitude towards God. In this way, like Job, we can receive both good and difficult gifts without sinning against God.

Third, our self worth is defined by who we are in Christ, not the things that we possess. As prosperity has exploded worldwide in the past 75 years, corporate advertisers have worked hard to convince us that our personal worth is determined by our net worth. Nearly every commercial in either print or broadcast mediums utilizes rhetoric that links our sense of personal value to our possessions. It is not surprising, therefore, that most of the people in our world pursue wealth as a means of personal fulfillment.

As we saw yesterday, however, Jesus provides a different picture entirely. "Take guard against all covetousness, for one's life does not consist in the abundance of his possessions (Lk 12:13-21)." This truth statement is linked to the parable of the rich farmer. Although God had favored him with a huge harvest, he did not consider God or his kingdom when he thought about his newfound wealth. Instead, he planned to build bigger barns so he could hoard his wealth. God describes this man as a "fool," who will die and leave his wealth to others. The point of Jesus' parable is clear—wealth is simply a tool to be used for kingdom endeavors; it is not the measure one's personal value and identity.

As James wrote to his church, he was reinforcing this truth about money. Money is not the measure of one's value to God or his church. This is why he will write later that the rich should not be given the places of prominence in the local church (2:1-10). James is teaching us that our personal portfolios do not determine our significance in Christ. If we are poor by the world's standards, we should boast in the riches that we have in Christ. If we are rich by the world's standards, we should boast in our humility, understanding that our financial blessings are on loan to us for use in God's kingdom.

We will never experience true contentment until we understand that we have significance in life solely on the basis of our personal relationship with God. It is God who gives our lives value, not the temporary trinkets of this world. He alone is at work in us to accomplish his purpose in our lives (Phil 2:13).

Fourth, our life's purpose is to pursue the glory of God and his righteousness, knowing that we can trust his sovereign plan for our lives. When we read this statement, it may give us pause. In fact, it may be that as you read this today, this statement does not reflect the current vision of your life. Like most people, you may have your own ideas about the ultimate purpose of your life. It may even reflect the plans of most people: get an education, find a good job, make a lot of money, accumulate the possessions that you believe will make you happy, retire early, and spend your final years playing in the sandbox of your choosing. There's just one problem with this particular plan—in no way does it resemble God's will for your life.

Instead, God wants you to abandon your plan and choose his. What is his plan, you ask? His plan looks like this: accept Jesus as your personal Savior and Lord, deny yourself and surrender your life plans to his sovereign leadership, take up his cross and follow him, and embrace his kingdom purposes for your life (Lk 9:23-26; Mt 11:28-29; Mt 6:33). As you can see, this is a very different plan for your life than the world suggests.

Of course, you may be tempted to stay on your current path. After all, fear may dissuade you from following God by faith into his purpose for your life. In the end, however, your choice will determine whether you accomplish God's will or waste your life. You may indeed attain all of the money and possessions you desire, but then you will suffer the awful consequences mentioned by Jesus: "What does it profit a man if he gains the whole world and loses or forfeits himself (Lk 9:25)." Most of the wealthiest individuals in human history have died without Christ and stepped into a cursed eternity without him. What did their wealth provide them but a few years of comfort?

Instead, God calls you to embrace the truth of James 1:12. God wants you to live for his glory and pursue his kingdom purpose for your life. He wants you to follow him wherever he leads, knowing that you will receive the crown of life, both now and in the life to come.

We accomplish this by learning and living these truths: God is sovereign over all of the circumstances in our lives, both good and bad; everything we possess in this life is a gift of God's grace; our self worth is defined upon the basis of our relationship with God, not our possessions; our purpose in life is to pursue the glory of God and his righteousness. We can trust his sovereign plans for our lives, so live with joy!

Food for Thought

God's plan for our life and our plan for our life are often at odds. Spend some time today thinking about your life. What are your priorities? What are your long-term goals? To what degree does God's plan for your life intersect with your own? You have one precious, God-given life. How will you spend it? Will you strive to fulfill God's purpose and live in the reality of his favor? Or, will you seek your own path, only to discover that you've wasted your life?

Faith in Action

Do an honest appraisal of your life plan, including your goals and priorities. Ask if your plan lines up with God's plan. If not, consider ways to bring your life in line with God's purposes for you. You may need to talk with your pastor to receive help with this. If you are pursuing God with your life, think about new ways for your life to intersect with God's kingdom plans.

Prayer

Today, spend time talking with God about his purpose for your life. God created you uniquely to make a contribution to his kingdom. Have you surrendered to that? Perhaps that needs to be the focus of your prayer time. Or, perhaps you need to ask God for continued clarity about his purpose for your life. Finally, thank God for the privilege to know and serve him with your life, and ask him for divine appointments today to make a difference in his kingdom!

James 1:13-16

Let no one say when he is tempted, "I am being tempted by God," for God cannot be tempted with evil, and he himself tempts no one. But each person is tempted when he is lured and enticed by his own desire. Then desire when it has conceived gives birth to sin, and sin when it is fully grown brings forth death. Do not be deceived, my beloved brothers.

Sin is the great enemy of our hearts. It has the potential to destroy relationships, tarnish reputations, manipulate motives, and numb spiritual passion. The Bible is full of stories about people just like us who learned firsthand both the power and consequence of sin. Abraham lied about his marriage, and his wife Sarah was taken into the harem of a pagan king. Jacob deceived his father to steal his brother's birthright, and his brother wanted to kill him. David committed adultery with Bathsheba, and then arranged to have her husband killed in battle, dooming himself to a life of turmoil. Peter denied Jesus when he was on trial for his life, and his failure nearly derailed his ministry.

There is a common thread that runs through every one of these stories. In each instance, there was a moment of truth when a temptation brought each person to the brink of sin. Abraham was tempted to lie when he was confronted by fear. Jacob was tempted to steal when he was confronted by greed. David was tempted to lust when he was confronted by a beautiful woman. Peter was tempted to deny Jesus when he was confronted by ridicule. This was

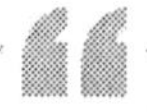

Webster defines the word "tempt" like this: "To entice to do wrong by promise of pleasure or gain."

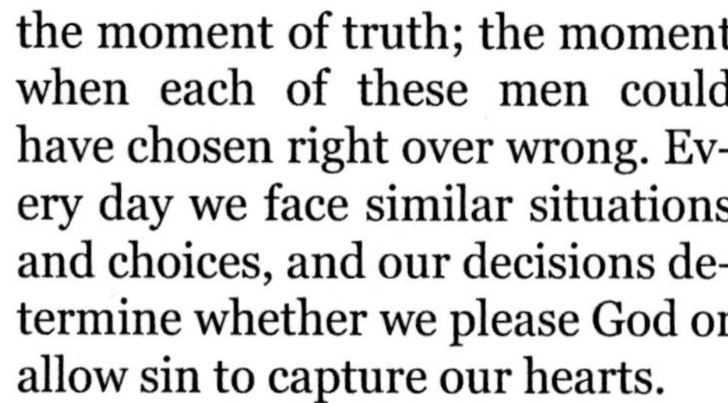

the moment of truth; the moment when each of these men could have chosen right over wrong. Every day we face similar situations and choices, and our decisions determine whether we please God or allow sin to capture our hearts.

In today's text, we learn about temptation and how it serves as the gateway for sin. James is continuing his discussion about the reality of personal trials, specifically the trial of financial hardship. Every day, the lowly brother (1:9) is tempted to covet the possessions of the wealthy rather than boast in his exaltation in Christ. Similarly, the rich brother is tempted daily to place his confidence in his wealth rather than boast in God's grace. In both instances, yielding to this temptation produces sin, and this sin has the potential to damage both the people involved and God's kingdom. So, James is about to challenge both the rich and the poor brother to understand the longterm effects of succumbing to temptation. The truth in this passage relates to any type of personal trial or temptation that we may face, however. It is not limited to the example that James was addressing in his church. As we look at this text today, we will discover some valuable principles about overcoming temptation.

First, temptation results from the interaction of our fallen nature with a fallen world. Webster defines the word "tempt" like this: "To entice to do wrong by promise of pleasure or gain." There are several truths about temptation that we must understand as we study this text. First, temptation itself is not sin. The Bible says that Jesus was tempted during his time on earth, but he never sinned by yielding to temptation (Heb 4:15). When we invite Jesus into our lives by faith, we become a new creation in Christ (2 Cor 5:17). However, we carry the shadow of our old, fallen nature with us until the day we are perfected in the presence of God in heaven. Until then, our old, fallen nature makes us susceptible to the temptations of a fallen world (Rom 7:15-25).

This is exactly what James is talking about in this text. God is never the source of the temptation to sin. He may allow us to encounter trials, as we saw in 1:2-4, but he cannot tempt us with sin for two reasons. First, because of the perfection of his character, he cannot be tempted to sin, nor can he sin (Titus 1:2). Second, James says, "He tempts no one with sin." When we face temptation, it is never the result of God's activity.

Where does temptation come from, then? James answers our question: "Each person is tempted when he is lured and enticed by his own desire." There are three important words here for us to understand. The most important word in this phrase is "desire." It is often translated "lust" in the Bible. In the Bible, lust means "misdirected passion." God made us to be passionate people. We can be passionate about many things in a good and godly way. For instance, I can use my finances in a way that honors Christ and reflects good stewardship. But, if my passions are misdirected in this area, greed can become a dangerous enemy (1 Tim 6:9-10). This is the definition of lust.

The next important word is "lured." It means to be carried away by desire. It's a word that suggests being drawn away from a place of safety. The third important word is the word "enticed." This word means to be captured or trapped. Now, imagine you're standing up to your ankles in a fast moving river, the kind I've fished numerous times in Montana. You've already fished the places close to you, but there is a spot out in the middle where you really want to cast your fly. In this scenario, the desire for that huge fish begins to lure you from the safety of the shallows to the danger of the rapids. Once you walk out into the swirling waters, you're quickly trapped by its deadly force.

What's interesting to note here is that *you're* ultimately the source of the temptation. The river isn't responsible—it's warning you everywhere you look. The trout isn't responsible either—it's not his fault that he's a beautiful

Sin is anything that we do that displeases God and fails to honor him.

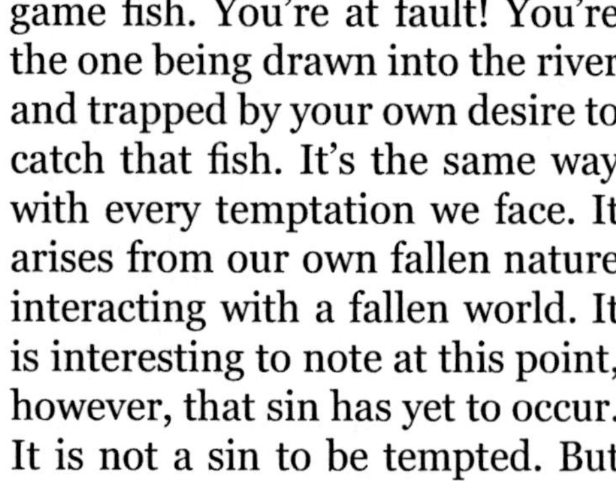

game fish. You're at fault! You're the one being drawn into the river and trapped by your own desire to catch that fish. It's the same way with every temptation we face. It arises from our own fallen nature interacting with a fallen world. It is interesting to note at this point, however, that sin has yet to occur. It is not a sin to be tempted. But as James will note next, when temptation is present, sin is always lurking nearby.

Second, sin results from the interaction of our fallen nature and temptation. James teaches us that temptation is a byproduct of our own fallen desires. Notice 1:15a, "Then desire when it has conceived gives birth to sin." As we saw earlier, desire, or misdirected passion, is our enemy. James uses the picture of the birthing process to help us understand how desire works. We are in the middle of temptation when our sinful desires lure and entice us towards sin. Often, however, we don't act on temptation right away. While God wants us to escape the temptation by running to him in prayer, we may choose to begin thinking about the temptation, all the while beginning to rationalize why acting on it would be ok. James likens this to pregnancy. He uses the word "conceive" to describe it. A woman is pregnant for nine months before she gives birth. Similarly, when desire produces temptation, we may choose to indulge it in our minds. Then, after time spent conceiving it, sin becomes a reality in our life through action.

Consider our fishing analogy one more time. You may be tempted to go into the fast moving water because you are lured and enticed by the lunker trout. Wisdom would be shouting to you to simply walk away. But perhaps you can't hear wisdom because of the roar being made by the rushing waters. So, you stand there letting the thought of catching that fish grow in your mind until you throw the moment of sinful action; it has the potential to produce both spiritual and physical death.

James uses the phrase "fully grown" to convey this truth. It's a phrase that means to achieve full potential. When sin reaches this point, the potential of death is very real. There is a warning here—every sin has the potential to kill something in your life. Sin can kill your health, your abilities, your dreams, your finances, your marriage, your family, and even you (Gal 6:7-8). These types of consequences don't occur immediately in most instances. For many, there may be years of sin before the reality of death becomes apparent.

Remember our illustration about fishing in the river? You may be willing to risk everything to catch that trout. You may even be able to wade into the river and fight against the current while you indulge the object of your desire. But one misstep, the shifting of one rock under your feet, and you will be swept away to certain death.

Despite the warning of this text, people reject its truth every day. That is why James ends his teaching with these words in 1:16: "Do not be deceived, my beloved brothers." That is the real danger when our sinful desires connect with a fallen world—we have the potential to deceive ourselves. We can convince ourselves that we are the one exception to this truth; we're the ones who will escape the consequences of our sin. This is a foolish deception indeed. Here is James' final equation of the process of sin: temptation + desire + incubation + sin = death. Every time we sin we travel through this process, and we risk death in our lives.

> *Temptation + Desire + Incubation + Sin = Death*

There is a remedy for this, however; a way to avoid the awful consequences of death in our lives. It's called confession. 1 John 1:9 says, "If we confess our sins, he is faithful and just to forgive us our sins and to cleanse us from all unrighteousness." All of us are caution to the wind and step out into the dangerous rapids, risking everything in the process.

This is the process of moving from temptation to sin. It can happen in our lives in many ways. It can happen to a student faced with the possibility of failing a test. He is tempted to cheat, but he knows it's really stealing. After thinking about it and weighing the options, however, he gives in to sin. He'd rather take his chances with cheating than fail a test. It can happen to a wife who becomes angry with her husband for treating her unkindly. All day she is tempted to get back at her husband. She reflects on all the things she wants to say, and by the time he gets home, she's ready to let him have it. She would rather risk harming the relationship than extend forgiveness. It can happen to a husband who feels frustrated at his job. He works hard but he never seems to be rewarded financially for his efforts. One day he is tempted to siphon a little money out of the company. He begins to think it over and soon he has devised a plan to embezzle some money. He would rather risk prison than feel unappreciated.

Each of these circumstances is an example of a temptation that becomes a sin. All that was necessary was the time required to conceive it. The word James uses for sin is the Greek word "harmartia." It's a word that means to "miss the mark." Sin is anything that we do that displeases God and fails to honor him. So here is the progression that James has described so far: temptation + desire + incubation = sin. But there is still one last step in the process of sin.

Third, death results from the consequences of our sin. Notice the second half of 1:15, "Sin when it is fully grown brings forth death." James continues the idea of the human birth process here. Life on earth begins at conception, is realized at birth, and continues until the moment of death. It is a process. So too is the process of sin. It becomes a possibility at the moment of temptation; it is conceived through the meditations of the heart; it is birthed at tempted, and sadly, we may choose to sin in that moment. It's what we do next that is so important. If we choose to enjoy and embrace our sin in disobedience to God's purpose, we will lose his blessing and risk death in some area of our lives. But, if we choose instead to repent of our sin and seek God's forgiveness, we will be spared from the awful consequences of habitual sin. And, we will learn to flee from temptation rather than allow sin to capture our hearts.

Food for Thought

Have you ever thought about the way sin grows in your life? What temptation are you facing in your life today? Have you been asking God to deliver you from that temptation or have you been thinking about how to indulge it? You have a choice to make today—you can continue to let that potential sin grow in your heart, or you can abandon it. Are you currently participating in a secret sin? Confess and abandon it today—don't be deceived—it will lead to death.

Faith in Action

Read 1 Cor 10:13 to conclude your study today. Think about the different ways you can escape temptation. Of course, prayer and daily time in the word are your best defenses. But, if you're struggling with a serious sin issue in your heart, perhaps you need to talk with a pastor or friend about getting help. There is safety in a multitude of counselors, so consider seeking some wise counsel today (Pr 24:6).

Prayer

Today, spend time talking with God about the temptations you've been experiencing in your life. He already knows about them, and he's ready to help you overcome them. God is pulling for you today! He wants you to succeed in your spiritual journey and bring him glory through your choices. So, talk with him about the things that you're struggling with—there's nothing better than the feeling of knowing that you're walking with God!

James 1:17-18

Every good gift and every perfect gift is from above, coming down from the Father of lights with whom there is no variation or shadow due to change. Of his own will he brought us forth by the word of truth, that we should be a kind of firstfruits of his creatures.

Gratitude is in short supply these days. Hold the door for someone and you'll rarely receive a "Thank you." Go the extra mile to help a stranger, and it won't be enough. And don't hold your breath waiting on an acknowledgment from the person you waved through at the four-way stop—you'll probably pass out before you get it!

Sadly, in our 21st century culture, an attitude of gratitude has been replaced by an attitude of entitlement. Webster defines entitlement as the belief that one is deserving of certain benefits or privileges. Where once people were grateful to have a door held for them, now they believe they deserve it. Where once people in distress was grateful for any kind of help, now they believe they should have the right to determine the scope of that help. And where once people were appreciative of other courteous drivers, now they demand the right of way—after all, they're entitled to it. As a result, there are few waves, "Thank yous," or words of appreciation. No one expresses gratitude for the things they believe they deserve.

Ours isn't the only culture that wrestles with gratitude issues, however. In fact, James was addressing this very issue in his own church. As you'll recall from 1:9-16, there were some tensions in the church between members

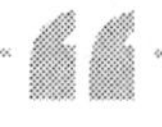

No one expresses gratitude for the things they believe they deserve.

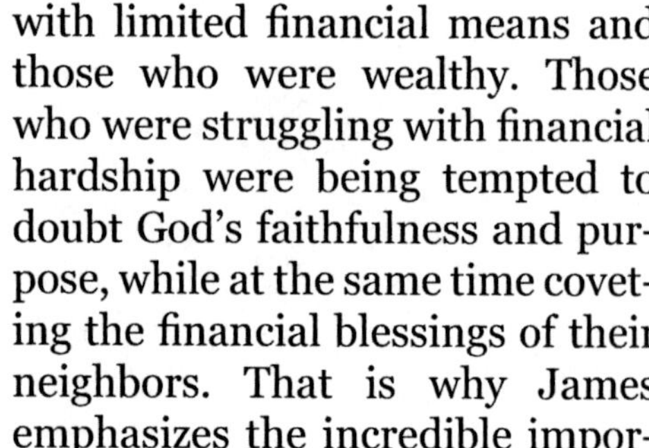

with limited financial means and those who were wealthy. Those who were struggling with financial hardship were being tempted to doubt God's faithfulness and purpose, while at the same time coveting the financial blessings of their neighbors. That is why James emphasizes the incredible importance of contentment in 1:12. He knew that contentment is the tangible expression of faith. It provides evidence that we trust both God and his provision for our needs.

James expands our understanding of this important concept in today's truth: Gratitude is the tangible expression of contentment. As we study these verses today, we must understand a couple of key ideas. First, God is the source of every good gift in our lives. James teaches us that God is in the business of giving good gifts to his kids. He describes these gifts as pleasant or excellent. These are the kind of gifts you love to get, not hand-me-downs or knock-offs. Why does he do this? Certainly not because we are entitled to them. God gives great gifts because he is a great giver. Ultimately, God gives good things to us because he is good.

Second, God will continue to give us good things in our lives because he never changes. James ends 1:17 by reminding us where our gifts originate. They come down "from the Father of lights with whom there is no variation or shadow due to change." Remember, these good gifts are not given to us as result of our own efforts or entitlement. They are the result of God's love, grace, and mercy in our lives. God never changes. He isn't like a shadow that bobs and weaves in response to the actions of others. He is faithful, consistent, and true. He is always in the process of giving us good things, because he is the source of every good thing in our lives.

There is one good gift that trumps all the others, however—it is the gift of salvation. Notice what James says about our salvation in 1:18, “Of his own will he brought us forth by the word of truth, that we should be a kind of firstfruits of his creatures.” In this verse we learn several exciting things about our salvation.

First, are saved because God willed to save us. James says, “Of his own will he brought us forth by the word of truth.” The plan of salvation originated with God. He created the plan in eternity past, accomplished the plan when his son Jesus died on the cross and was raised from the dead, and applied the plan to our lives when we placed our faith in Jesus (Eph 1:3-14). God “brings us forth” through the process of salvation. This is another reference to the birthing process. It’s the same phrase you saw in 1:15. Whereas sin brings forth death, salvation brings forth life. This is what Jesus is talking about when he tells Nicodemus that he must be “born again (Jn 3:3).”

Second, the process of being “born again” to spiritual life requires both a knowledge and acceptance of the gospel. Quite simply, the gospel requires three things of us: a) We must admit that we have sinned against a holy God, and we are deserving of his wrath; b) We must believe that Jesus died on the cross to pay the penalty for our sin, and he was raised from the dead to confirm God’s acceptance of his sacrifice; c) We must confess our sins to God and ask for his forgiveness, while surrendering our hearts to Jesus as Lord. The gospel is the “word of truth” that God uses to save us from our sins.

Once we are saved, God begins a transformation process in our hearts and lives. James says this saving process makes us “a kind of firstfruits of his creatures.” This is what Paul is referring to when he writes, “If anyone is in Christ, he is a new creation. The old has passed away; behold, the new has come (2 Cor 5:17). Once we have a personal relationship with God through faith in Jesus, we have the potential to

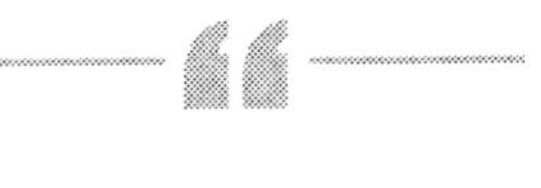

Gratitude is the tangible expression of contentment.

As long as we are discontent, we will always be ungrateful too.

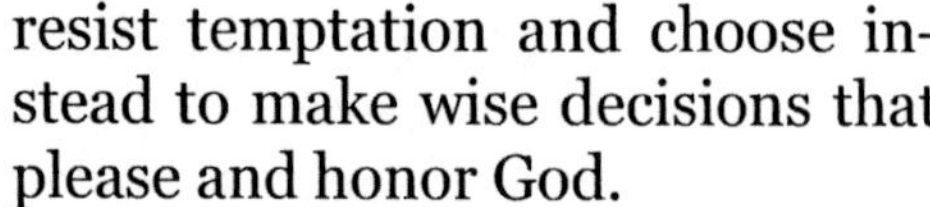

resist temptation and choose instead to make wise decisions that please and honor God.

One of the ways we can please and honor God is to live with an attitude of gratitude. Rather than feeling entitled to God's favor, gratitude expresses an appreciation for God's favor and the good gifts that result from it. Here is how contentment and gratitude work together in our lives. Every day, we are confronted with the temptation to be discontent. Like the people in James' church, we may be tempted to be discontent with our finances. We may look at people who have more money or possessions than us and be tempted to covet. Or, we may begin to wonder why God doesn't give us more.

Contentment, on the other hand, is an expression of our faith in God. It is a byproduct of trusting God to supply our needs in whatever manner he chooses and being satisfied with his provision (Phil 4:10-13). Contentment goes far beyond finances, however. God wants us to be content with all of the circumstances in our lives, including our marriages, families, jobs, health, church and even our opportunities. Once we begin to experience contentment, we are capable of being grateful to God for his good gifts.

Why is this important for our lives today? As long as we are discontent, we will always be ungrateful too. We will always feel as if we deserve more than we have. Contentment and gratitude come from realizing that God owes us nothing but judgment. As a result, every gift he chooses to give us is a good one. As we noted above, salvation is the gift we deserve least, and yet we have been given it as a gift from God. It's the greatest gift we will ever be given, and we should overflow with a sense of gratitude every time we think about it.

We have received all of the other good gifts in our lives from God as well. The blessing of friendship and familial relationship is a good gift from God. Our talents are a good gift from God. The provision of our daily bread is a good gift from God, as is the many ways in which God shepherds us on a daily basis. Finally, the granting of the desires of our hearts is a good gift from God as well.

Every day we have a choice to make about whether to be content or discontent in our lives. We have to choose whether to be grateful or ungrateful to God for his good gifts. Today, let's choose to practice contentment and to express gratitude to God for his good gifts—especially the gift of salvation!

Food for Thought

How would you describe your life today? Are you content with God's provision or are you wrestling with discontentment in some area of your life? Have you expressed gratitude to God for his good gifts lately, or are you upset with God for some perceived lack of his favor in your life? If you're struggling with discontentment and ingratitude in your life today, spend some time thinking about where those feelings are originating. Read James 1:12-16 again and assess where you are in the "temptation + desire + incubation + sin = death" process. What decisions do you need to make today? Choose contentment and gratitude in your life today!

Faith in Action

Spend some time today making a list of all of God's good gifts in your life. Be specific, and list as many as possible. Focusing on God's good gifts will help produce contentment and gratitude in your life, even if you're experiencing a trial in your life.

Prayer

If you have been allowing discontentment and ingratitude to rule your heart, confess that sin and turn from it today. Review your list of God's good gifts and lift a prayer of gratitude and praise for each one.

James 1:19-21

Know this, my beloved brothers: let every person be quick to hear, slow to speak, slow to anger; for the anger of man does not produce the righteousness of God. Therefore put away all filthiness and rampant wickedness and receive with meekness the implanted word, which is able to save your souls.

When was the last time something made you angry? If you're like me, you can probably remember everything about it—what happened, why it got under your skin, how you responded, and how sorry you felt about it later. That's the thing about anger—it can appear in an instant, but we carry its consequences around with us for a long time.

As James continues to write his book, he challenges his church to get serious about their anger issues. He doesn't tell us if he's referring to someone or something in particular. Maybe some of his folks were angry with God because they didn't have as much money as they wanted (1:9-16). Or, perhaps he just knew that anger is a dangerous enemy, and it lurks within every human heart.

Regardless, he provides us with some great truths about how to escape the temptation of anger. His first truth is this: Anger works against the purposes of God in our lives. Notice this phrase, "The anger of man does not produce the righteousness of God." James is teaching us that God wants us to

Anger works against the purposes of God in our lives.

Anger is a control issue.

be righteous people. He wants our lives to reflect his character and values. When we become angry, we lose sight of this. Instead of modeling God's righteousness, we let our sinful nature take control with all of its fury.

When I was a boy, I enjoyed reading comic books. One interesting comic book hero is the Hulk. In the story, Dr. Bruce Banner is a physicist who is exposed to gamma radiation. As a result, he develops the ability to transform into the Hulk, a green monster who leaves destruction in his wake. Interestingly, Dr. Banner turns into the Hulk when he becomes angry. And, when the Hulk manifests, Dr. Banner cannot control him.

Every one of us has a Hulk inside our hearts just waiting to emerge. He waits until we are angry, and then he manifests himself in all of his fury. We may foolishly believe that we can control him, but that's just wishful thinking. We are reckless when we become angry; reason, logic, and spiritual discipline disappear as the monster takes control. Our unique anger-monster may manifest itself in different ways. For some of us, it may result in yelling, cursing, and the occasional broken dish. For others, it may be the quiet rage that can slay someone without saying a word. But every time, just like Dr. Banner when he reverts back to his human form, we are left with painful regrets and a mess to clean up.

So, how does anger work? Anger is a control issue. We all like to be in control of our circumstances. When our control is threatened, we get angry. This can happen in numerous ways. Have you ever been standing in a long line at a concession stand during a college football game? You're patiently waiting your turn, and then some yahoo walks up and cuts in line about 10' in front of you? Do you remember how that made you feel? Have you ever made plans for the weekend only to discover that your boss has changed the schedule and you now have to work? How did you respond to that? Have you ever had a discussion with your spouse, and he or she questioned the wisdom of your plans? Can you recall the emotions you felt in that situation?

Each of these situations has the potential to make us angry, because we feel like someone is taking away our control. When we feel like this, our emotions begin to engage, and we begin to feel angry. The first evidence of this will be over-reactive speech. Even though we may not have all of the information we need to make a wise decision (i.e., the guy didn't really cut in line, he had left briefly to use the restroom, and someone was holding his spot), we're ready to mouth off about the nerve of someone challenging our control.

Usually by this point, anger is blossoming into a full-blown event. This is the danger zone. This is the point where temptation becomes sin. We may say and do things that we regret, not just for a moment, but for a lifetime. Clearly, James knows what he is talking about when he says, "The anger of man does not produce the righteousness of God." This is why he tells us to "put away all filthiness and rampant wickedness." This is a great description of anger—it is filthy and wicked, and it's at the root of every violent conversation and action (Mt 5:21-26).

Thankfully, James offers us an alternative course of action when we are tempted to become angry. It's a three-part process. He writes, "Let every person be quick to hear, slow to speak, slow to anger." When our control is threatened, we begin planning our retaliation strategy before we even allow ourselves to process the information in a way that honors Christ.

Occasionally, my wife Lyla will remind me of my tendency to become preoccupied with ministry responsibilities to the detriment

"Let every person be quick to hear, slow to speak, slow to anger."

Left unchecked, anger will destroy all it touches.

of our relationship. This means that I'm present physically but my mind is elsewhere. I have two possible reactions when she makes this observation. My instinctual reaction is to become defensive. Rather than hearing what she has to say, I launch into the reasons why she's wrong, all the while trying to defend my actions. Of course, we both know that I'm wrong. The more I try to deflect the truth, the more anger has a chance to build up in my heart. In those moments I may be tempted to say things that are hurtful to her. Clearly, this doesn't accomplish anything that would build our relationship.

Our text today reveals that I can choose a different, Spirit-motivated reaction, however. Rather than give in to my anger, I should react with grace. Because I know that my wife loves me and wants the best for me, I should trust that she is telling me the truth. I should value her insight and perspective—she knows me better than anyone, and she knows when my mind has checked out. Then, I should speak with grace. I should be honest with her, and myself, by simply admitting that I'm distracted. I should ask for her forgiveness and turn my attention back towards home—my ministry responsibilities can wait for another time. A response like this will eliminate anger, and the chaos it produces, every time.

James concludes with one final word of admonition for defeating anger, however. He writes, "Receive with meekness the implanted word, which is able to save your souls." Here, he is reinforcing the importance of embracing the wisdom found in God's word. He uses an interesting word to make his point. It's the word "meekness." This word is the opposite of anger. It means "power under control." Anger is an abuse of power; it's out of control. Meekness is the opposite. When we are meek, it means that we are submitting our lives to the control of the Holy Spirit.

It results from accepting the truth about anger: it is filthy and wicked, and it has the potential to destroy every good thing in our lives. When we receive this truth rightly, it will transform the way we respond to control issues, and it will produce the righteousness of God in us.

Food for Thought

Everyone wrestles with anger at different times and in different ways. Sometimes it's an anger that explodes; other times it is a passive/aggressive anger that is revealed in non-verbal ways. Both types are devastating to relationships. Do you wrestle with anger? If so, what kind of anger do you experience? What are the things that make you angry? How do you respond when you get angry? In what ways is anger damaging you and the people around you? Left unchecked, anger will destroy all it touches. God stands ready to help you in this area as you let his word speak truth into your life today.

Faith in Action

We get angry when our personal control is threatened in some way. Today, be on guard against the things that trigger your anger most often. Prepare yourself in advance to respond to those triggers differently. When they occur, be "quick to hear, slow to speak, and slow to anger." God will bless your obedience, and you will become a blessing to others.

Prayer

As you spend time in prayer today, talk with God about any struggles you may have with anger. Confess the sin of anger where necessary (and later confess that sin to the person you were angry with). Ask the Holy Spirit to help you walk in meekness—power under control. Ask God to help you see that rejecting anger leads to his blessing in your life.

James 1:22-24

But be doers of the word, and not hearers only, deceiving yourselves. For if anyone is a hearer of the word and not a doer, he is like a man who looks intently at his natural face in a mirror. For he looks at himself and goes away and at once forgets what he was like.

There are many character traits that contribute to success: honesty, hard work, discipline, and perseverance are just a few. But one character trait is foundational for all of these—being teachable. I've lived long enough to observe the successes and failures of thousands of people. One thing always separates people into one of these two categories; their ability to heed instruction.

I served as a police officer in Chattanooga, TN, for three years after I graduated from college. I dealt almost exclusively with people who refused to follow instructions. One night I was called to a young woman's apartment. When I arrived, I observed a former boyfriend harassing her. After speaking with him for several minutes, I advised him to leave and not return. He appeared to comply with my request, and disappeared towards the parking lot. I left the scene, but 20 minutes later I received a call to return to the young ladies apartment. When I returned, the young man was back at her door repeating his harassment. This time, as I encouraged him to leave I provided him with

We are hardwired by sin to believe that we know the best choices to make for our lives.

God's word functions like a mirror; it exposes us to what we look like spiritually at any given time.

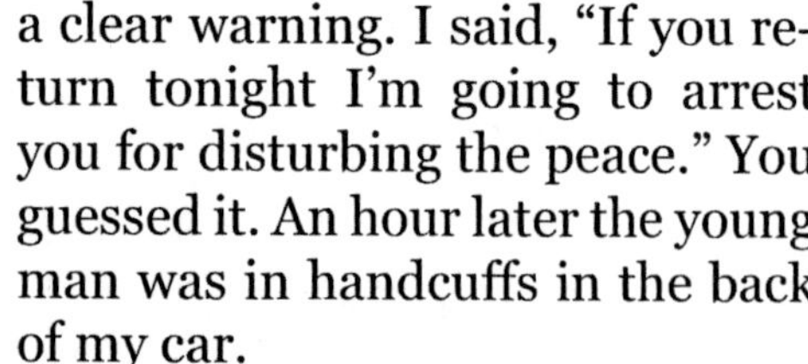

a clear warning. I said, "If you return tonight I'm going to arrest you for disturbing the peace." You guessed it. An hour later the young man was in handcuffs in the back of my car.

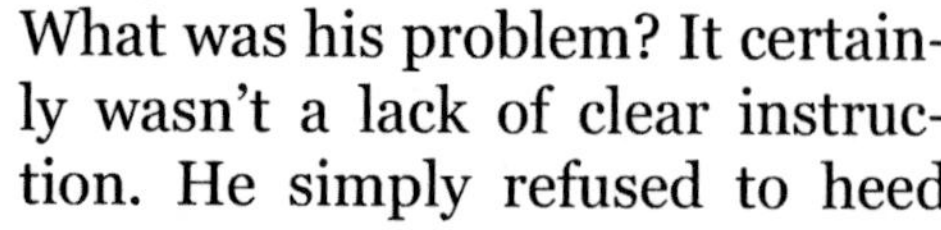

What was his problem? It certainly wasn't a lack of clear instruction. He simply refused to heed the instruction. Today, I serve as an adjunct professor for a prominent Baptist seminary. My classes provide clear and specific project assignments, along with the corresponding grading rubrics. Yet I routinely grade papers from students who simply refuse to follow the directions. Often, they try and explain that the method they chose is actually superior to the requirements. Again, the problem isn't an ability to understand the directions—it's an unwillingness to follow them.

There is something buried deep within our sinful natures that resists submitting to the authority of others. We are hardwired by sin to believe that we know the best choices to make for our lives. God knows our weakness in this area better than anyone. In today's text, James tackles the problem head-on and provides us with some great words of instruction and warning.

In yesterday's devotion, James provided us with the key to overcoming the sin of anger (and it applies to other types of sin too): "Receive with meekness the implanted word, which is able to save your souls." Ultimately, the key to success is our ability to receive the instruction of God's word with a teachable spirit.

How do we do that? James gives us the answer: "Be doers of the word, and not hearers only, deceiving yourselves." When we approach God's word with a teachable spirit, we hear with a goal of applying the truth to our lives. But if we read the Bible with an unteachable spirit, we are "hearers only." This phrase was used to refer to listening to music at a concert. We enjoy it while it's happening, but when we leave we quickly forget what we've heard.

James provides us with a great illustration of this. He talks about a guy looking at himself in a mirror. We look into mirrors on multiple occasions everyday. It begins when we're getting dressed in the morning and concludes when we're brushing our teeth before bed. Each time, we look at ourselves. Sometimes, if we're trying to get something out of our eye, we may gaze intently into the mirror. Other times, we may simply glance at the mirror to make sure our hair looks right. Regardless, a universal phenomenon occurs once we've left the company of our reflection in the mirror—we forget what we look like. I've been looking in mirrors for 50 years now. I still struggle with this.

James teaches us that this same phenomenon occurs when we read the Bible. God's word functions like a mirror; it exposes us to what we look like spiritually at any given time. If we're teachable, we will look intently at that image and allow it to impact our spiritual appearance. If we're stubborn, however, we will simply glance at God's truth and then leave unchanged.

James warns us that a great danger accompanies this choice. If we refuse to be teachable we expose ourselves to the potential of self-deception. The word James uses in verse 22 means "to deceive by false reasoning or to delude oneself." There are two ways that we can do this. First, we can deceive ourselves into thinking that sins like anger are not as devastating as they truly are. Second, we can delude ourselves into believing that our own plans are better than God's plans for us. Both of these are flawed premises based upon sinful, human reasoning.

Rather than pursue this flawed approach to decision making, God wants us to be teachable! This begins with the simple acceptance of one key idea—God's truth

God's truth is always right and always best.

is always right and always best. When we submit to God's truth with a teachable spirit, we position ourselves to experience God's favor and blessing. In Proverbs 1:7 God says, "The fear of the Lord is the beginning of knowledge; fools despise wisdom and instruction." It is foolish to be a hearer of the word, yet turn from it and ignore its truth. It is wise to be both a hearer and an obedient doer of the word.

Food for Thought

Ultimately, our success in every area of life is defined by the degree to which we are teachable. If you had to determine your own willingness to be teachable on a scale of 1 to 10 (with one being worst and 10 being best), what number would you give yourself? Think about some times in your life when being stubborn had a negative impact on you. What would you do differently if you had the chance to repeat the decision today? Using the same scale, how teachable are you when you hear or study God's word? Has God taught you something this month in your study of James that you're refusing to hear and obey? What is it and how does God want you to respond?

Faith in Action

Today, pay special attention to the opportunities you have to be teachable. This may occur at home, on your job, or in some other area of your life. Being teachable involves four distinct steps: a) listening; b) reflecting; c) practicing; d) applying. Work to apply these four steps when learning something new. You can use these same steps when applying God's truth to your life too.

Prayer

In your prayer time today, talk with God about this important subject. Be honest with him about your challenges with being teachable. Ask him for help in hearing and doing the things he is teaching you in your study of James.

James 1:25

But the one who looks into the perfect law of liberty, and perseveres, being no hearer who forgets but a doer who acts, he will be blessed in his doing.

Recently, I was taking a walk around my farm enjoying the beauty of a fall day. The air was cool, the leaves were beginning to turn to soft shades of rust and umber, and my dogs were romping through the pasture. As I walked along the wood line, my eyes were drawn down towards a strange looking piece of wood. Immediately, I stopped to examine it as it lay amidst the fallen leaves. To my surprise, it was a snake!

I rarely see snakes out during the fall, and this snake appeared to be in no hurry to move. So, I bent down and began to examine it closely, It was bluish-gray in color and had the most amazing rectangular markings. What made it so pretty was the orange dorsal stripe that ran along its back. Its head was not shaped like a triangle, so I had no fear that it was poisonous. I've rarely had the opportunity to get that close to a snake in its natural habitat. I later discovered that it was a Hog Nose snake, which is very common here in South Carolina. My willingness to take the time to study this beautiful snake allowed me to discover its true identity and to learn much about its habitat and habits. It's a valuable snake to have on the farm.

As we look at today's text, James is going to challenge us to approach God's word with the same sense of interest, expectation, and teachable spirit. As we saw yesterdary, our spiritual success is determined ultimately by our willingness to be both hearers and doers of biblical truth. Today's text reveals the benefits that we will receive through obedience.

> *God's truth is perfect, because God is perfect.*

James writes, "The one who looks into the perfect law… will be blessed in his doing." The phrase "looks into" describes perfectly my encounter with old Mr. Hog Nose. When I saw him, I bent over to see, stooped down to examine, and then made a great discovery. This is the way God wants us to approach his word. Rather than hear and forget, like the man looking in the mirror, he wants us to spend time exploring and discovering its truth. This pursuit comes with an amazing promise attached. God promises that we will be blessed "in our doing." In other words, God will bless the choices we make in obedience to his word!

Many people ask this question: "How is God's word capable of leading to blessing in my life?" James answers that question for us. He describes God's word as "the perfect law, the law of liberty." Here, he emphasizes a key aspect of God's word—it contains truth. Twice he uses the word "law." In this context, it is referring to the whole truth of God, not simply the laws that are contained in the Pentateuch. God's word has value because it reveals his precepts and principles for living.

This isn't partial truth, however. James says it is "perfect." This word means to be without flaws. This speaks to the character of the one who has given us this truth—God himself. God's truth is perfect, because God is perfect. As a result, it speaks truth into every area of our lives, and we can trust it. God's precepts and principles, rooted as they are in his character, are always best for us.

They are best for us, because they lead to freedom in our lives. Sin is our biggest enemy, and we all possess a bent towards indulging the desires of the flesh (Gal 5:16-

24). The word "liberty" as it is used here means the capacity to be freed from the control of sinful choices and consequences—the very things that have the power to enslave and destroy us. God's perfect word equips us to make choices that result in God's blessings on our lives.

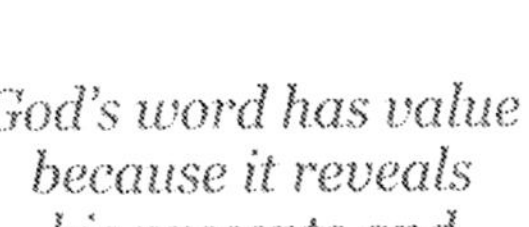

God's word has value because it reveals his precepts and principles for living.

One question remains, however: How do we do this? James teaches us that it is a daily process of hearing and obeying. He uses the word "perseveres" to help us understand. This Greek word means "to remain beside or continue always near." As you can see, it carries with it the understanding of consistent attention. When I think about this word, it makes me think of a mother sitting by the bed of a sick child. She will not leave her child's side until she is well. In the same way, we must consistently be attentive to God's word. We do this by spending time in the Bible everyday. When we persevere in our commitment to learn and follow God's truth, we will begin to develop God's character in our lives and to make wise choices that honor him. These choices will lead to success and blessing.

This truth is demonstrated in several ways throughout the first chapter of James. First, hearing and obeying God's word is a prerequisite for salvation. We cannot be born again until we believe and accept the gospel of Jesus Christ (1:21). Second, hearing and obeying God's word protects us from the harmful consequences of our sins. God always extends forgiveness, but he never promises to remove the consequences of our sin (1:15). Third, hearing and obeying God's word preserves our capacity to experience and enjoy God's blessings. God's word reinforces this truth in both the Old and New Testaments—obedience leads to God's favor; disobedience leads to God's discipline (1:25). Fourth, and finally, hearing and obeying God's truth prepares us to accomplish the specific kingdom work for which God created and saved us (1:27).

God's perfect word equips us to make choices that result in God's blessings on our lives.

As a result, we must make a daily commitment to "look into the perfect law, the law of liberty, and persevere." That's where a resource like 30 Days to the Bible can be so valuable for us. It provides us with a systematic and manageable approach to daily study. Every day we have the opportunity to encounter and apply God's truth to our lives. Every month, we can study a new book of the Bible, expanding our understanding of God's amazing book!

Food for Thought

The fact that you're reading this book is evidence that you have a desire to do exactly what James is teaching in today's text—learn and obey God's word. The practice of daily devotion through study and prayer is critical to your development as an effective disciple. If we're not careful, however, we may let other things get in the way of our time with God. What, if anything, has the potential to distract you from persevering in your personal devotion to God?

Faith in Action

This is day 12 of your study through James. Already, you've had a chance to hear some great truths. Spend some time today identifying the most important things God has taught you so far. Then, assess the degree to which you've been striving to apply those truths to your life.

Prayer

As you talk with God today, ask him to continue to grow within you a love for his word and the desire to obey it. Rejoice in the promise of his blessing as you follow after him today.

James 1:26-27

If anyone thinks he is religious and does not bridle his tongue but deceives his heart, this person's religion is worthless. Religion that is pure and undefiled before God, the Father, is this: to visit orphans and widows in their affliction, and to keep oneself unstained from the world.

Have you ever met someone who seemingly has no filter for his or her speech? I've met a number of people like that during my more than 25 years of ministry as a local church pastor. I remember one such woman from the first church I ever served. She was in charge of selecting the flowers that sat on the Lord's Supper table at the front of the worship center every Sunday morning. While that may seem like a small task, to her, it was the most important decision that was made every week in our church. On one occasion, the flowers had to be moved to make way for a special event. You would have thought that the church staff had denied the deity of Christ! She cornered us in a church hallway and blessed us with a profanity-laced tirade. Looking back, I'm sure she felt very religious arranging her flowers every week. But her vicious, angry speech revealed the true character of her heart.

True religion is not defined by our external activities; it is defined by our internal attitudes.

Today's verses conclude the section of teaching that James began in 1:19. As you remember, James teaches us to understand that anger is a devastating sin in our lives. It can manifest itself in many ways, but often it is revealed through hurtful, hateful speech; speech that reveals the rampant wickedness of our hearts. To counter the sin of anger, James challenges us to look intently into the perfect law of liberty, God's word, which alone can free us from sin—including the sin of anger.

In verses 26-27, James closes his discussion with a sober warning—true religion is not defined by our external activities; it is defined by our internal attitudes. In verse 26, he identifies self-control, or the lack thereof, as a primary indicator of spiritual maturity. Remember the lady from my first church? You could put her picture beside this verse, because she was the person James was talking about. If you asked her, she would have responded that she was very religious. After all, she arranged the flowers at the church every week. But God would have a different opinion of her. Rather than describing her as religious, he would describe her brand of religion as "worthless." In the Greek, this word means "empty or fake." You see, while her actions said one thing, her attitudes said something totally different. She was an angry woman who spouted angry words at anyone who got in her way. She had long since abandoned the truth of James 1:19. Like the man who looks into the mirror but then forgets what he looks like, she deceived herself into believing that religious activity equals spiritual maturity (1:22-24). Nothing could be further from the truth.

Thankfully, James provides a beautiful picture of authentic religion, the kind God loves, in verse 27. It is one of the clearest, most succinct portraits of spiritual maturity in the entire Bible. He begins by stating that there is a type of religious worship that is "pure and undefiled" before God the Father. These words mean to be clean and unpolluted, like a beautiful moun-

> *It is the pursuit of holiness that protects us from the blemish of sins.*

tain stream. Here, true religious worship is compared to the worthless religious activities of sinful people, whose ungodly hearts are revealed through angry, unbridled speech.

> *We bring glory to God when we show mercy to those with the greatest needs from a pure heart that is surrendered to God's truth.*

James identifies two specific choices made by authentic, religious worshipers. First, they cultivate a servant's heart. While anger is always a by-product of selfishness, authentic worshipers are selfless in their service of others. Specifically, James mentions the care of widows and orphans. These two groups represent the most vulnerable people in society. They are truly "afflicted." This word means to be crushed by difficult circumstances. Neither widows nor orphans can survive apart from the selfless care of others. And because they have the greatest needs, they are least capable of repaying the acts of service they receive. This really tests people's motives. Sadly, many people serve only in situations where they have the potential to receive something in return, even if it's simply the affirmation of others. Authentic worshippers, on the other hand, look for approval from only one source—God. As a result, they find joy in serving those who can offer them nothing in return.

Second, religious worshippers cultivate a pure heart. The entire book of James is devoted to this process of personal sanctification. In chapter one alone we've seen the following ingredients that contribute to developing a pure heart:

- Steadfastness (v. 3)
- Wisdom (v. 5)
- Humility (v. 9)
- Resisting temptation (v. 13-15)
- Self control (v. 19)
- Obedience to the word (v. 22)
- Perseverance in the study of the word (v. 25)

God has called us to live lives of compassion and justice.

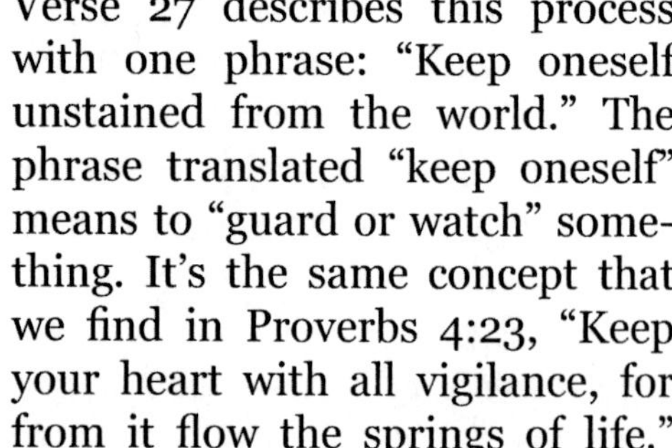

Verse 27 describes this process with one phrase: "Keep oneself unstained from the world." The phrase translated "keep oneself" means to "guard or watch" something. It's the same concept that we find in Proverbs 4:23, "Keep your heart with all vigilance, for from it flow the springs of life." This proverb describes guarding one's heart from the influence of the world's temptations. This is James' point exactly. Cultivating a pure heart requires intentionality; it is the pursuit of holiness that protects us from the blemish of sins like anger. Ultimately, it is a by-product of a consistent commitment to study and obey God's truth in all of the areas of our lives.

James' principle for us today is this: God has called us to live lives of compassion and justice. He echoes the words of the prophet Zechariah, "Thus says the LORD of hosts, Render true judgments, show kindness and mercy to one another, do not oppress the widow, the fatherless, the sojourner, or the poor, and let none of you devise evil against another in your heart (7:9-10)." We bring glory to God when we show mercy to those with the greatest needs from a pure heart that is surrendered to God's truth.

Food for Thought

All of us know people who hurt others because they have an unbridled tongue. Often, those people consider themselves to be religious. James says otherwise. Two things define those who are authentic worshipers: 1) They cultivate a servant's heart; 2) They cultivate a pure heart. How would describe yourself today? Has serving God become a regular part of your spiritual journey? Are you using your gifts for his glory to meet the needs of people in his church? What about the condition of your heart today? Are you striving daily to have victory over sin as you study and obey God's truth? What aspect of your life does God want to transform today?

Faith in Action

It's easy to substitute religious activity for spiritual growth. After all, spiritual growth takes time and effort. Spiritual growth is best determined through an honest assessment of our attitudes. Ultimately, our attitudes serve as the thermometer of our hearts. Spend time today assessing your attitudes. Why do you do what you do for the Lord? Do your motives reveal love or selfishness? Are you experiencing self-control or is anger predominant in your life? What does your speech say about your spiritual condition? Today, strive to allow the fruits of the Spirit to control your heart, speech, and activities for the glory of God.

Prayer

Today in your prayer time, open your heart up to the Lord in an intentional way. Ask God the Holy Spirit to examine your attitudes and speech. He will use the teaching from his word today to reveal if there are some attitudes or actions that are grieving him in these areas. If necessary, spend some time in personal confession and ask for his continued help in growing you as a spiritual worshiper.

James 2:1-13

My brothers, show no partiality as you hold the faith in our Lord Jesus Christ, the Lord of glory. For if a man wearing a gold ring and fine clothing comes into your assembly, and a poor man in shabby clothing also comes in, and if you pay attention to the one who wears the fine clothing and say, "You sit here in a good place," while you say to the poor man, "You stand over there," or, "Sit down at my feet," have you not then made distinctions among yourselves and become judges with evil thoughts? Listen, my beloved brothers, has not God chosen those who are poor in the world to be rich in faith and heirs of the kingdom, which he has promised to those who love him? But you have dishonored the poor man. Are not the rich the ones who oppress you, and the ones who drag you into court? Are they not the ones who blaspheme the honorable name by which you were called? If you really fulfill the royal law according to the Scripture, "You shall love your neighbor as yourself," you are doing well. But if you show partiality, you are committing sin and are convicted by the law as transgressors. For whoever keeps the whole law but fails in one point has become accountable for all of it. For he who said, "Do not commit adultery," also said, "Do not murder." If you do not commit adultery but do murder, you have become a transgressor of the law. So speak and so act as those who are to be judged under the law of liberty. For judgment is without mercy to one who has shown no mercy. Mercy triumphs over judgment.

> *God is not a respecter of persons.*

Have you ever noticed that it's easier to relate to people who are like us than people who are not? Our church participates in a community ministry that provides weekly assistance to the homeless. On a regular basis, we help provide meals and other resources for them. When I participate in this ministry, I am reminded of how prone I am to struggle with people who are different from me. The sights, the sounds, the smells, the dirt, and the desperate need—all of these things are so very foreign to me. Every time, I am forced to step out of my comfort zone to embrace those with the greatest needs among us.

The sinful condition of the human heart is constant across time. Just as I struggle to relate to the poor and weak in my culture, the people in James' church in Jerusalem did too. Like us, they were comfortable with people just like them—educated, upwardly mobile, and affluent. Consequently, they welcomed people into their lives and church who fit that description. However, our text today reveals that they struggled to identify with the poor man who came into their church.

But there is a deeper issue here; one that challenges us to look closely at the motives of our hearts. In the church in Jerusalem, James taught his people that they were in danger of marginalizing the poor man, and elevating the rich man, solely on the basis of their circumstances, not on the condition of their hearts. As a result, they were missing a very important truth in Scripture: God is not a respecter of persons. While man looks at the outward appearance, God always looks at the heart (1 Sam 16:7; Acts 10:34). And, while historically the social elite have ridiculed the gospel, it is the poor in spirit who embrace it and receive the kingdom of heaven (Mt 5:3).

The solution to this dangerous tendency in our lives is the pursuit of authentic mercy. In yesterday's study, we learned that authentic worshippers cultivate a servant's heart; they look for opportunities to show mercy to the people with the greatest needs—the poor. As James continues to develop that theme in today's text, the concept of authentic mercy is expanded to include the poor who attempt to gain access to the local church. James first principle is this: Authentic mercy rejects any favoritism on the basis of one's financial situation.

As the text continues, James provides us with the process for cultivating authentic mercy in our lives; it revolves around the great commandment. When Jesus was asked to identify the greatest commandment, he identified two: 1) love God with all of your heart; 2) love your neighbor as yourself (Mt 22:36-40). In verse eight, James focuses on the second commandment—loving our neighbor as ourselves. James second principle is this: Authentic mercy embraces the great commandment. He identifies it as the royal law, because King Jesus highlighted its importance for us. This law epitomizes what it means to demonstrate authentic mercy. It requires us to love everybody using the same scale—the love that we have for ourselves. Paul teaches us the same principle: "No one ever hated his own flesh, but nourishes and cherishes it (Eph 5:29)." As a result, whether we are talking about our wives, our children, our brothers and sisters in Christ, the wealthy or the poor, we should love everyone with the same passion and attention with which we love ourselves. When we love like this, we "do well."

Likewise, however, when we fail to love like this, and we show partiality to people who look like us at the expense of the poor, James says that we are sinning. Rather than being distributors of God's love and mercy, we become transgressors of God's truth. And, while this sin may seem small on our "sin meter," James reminds

> *Every sin we commit is a hindrance to God's work of sanctification in our lives and a hindrance to God's work through the gospel in the lives of others.*

The call to show mercy is the call to live out the gospel.

us that to be guilty of one sin is to be guilty of all. In other words, every sin we commit is a hindrance to God's work of sanctification in our lives and a hindrance to God's work through the gospel in the lives of others.

As James ends this section he references the two spiritual principles under discussion—self-controlled speech and authentic mercy. He writes, "So speak and so act as those who are to be judged under the law of liberty (2:12)." Clearly, James is teaching us that what we say and do have both temporal and eternal implications. In the here and now, our speech and actions greatly influence the spiritual well-being of others, either positively or negatively. In the hereafter, we must all give an account for our spiritual journey at the judgment seat of Christ. On that day, James reminds us that we will be judged according to the "law of liberty (1:25)." This is the law of the new covenant, the law of Christ, where love, grace, and mercy transform our lives and inform our words and deeds. This leads to James' third principle: Authentic mercy results in mercy.

At the judgment seat of Christ, we will each "receive what is due for what [we] have done in the body, whether good or evil (2 Cor 5:10)." While we will not be judged for our sins, we will be judged on the basis of our spiritual journey and the use of our spiritual gifts for God's glory. The result of this time of personal judgment will affect our eternal, spiritual rewards (1 Cor 3:10-15). However, James reveals that the pursuit and demonstration of authentic mercy to those around us, whether through self-control or the willingness to reject favoritism in the church, will lead to the favor of Christ on the Day of Judgment. He writes, "Mercy triumphs over judgment," because mercy eliminates the need for judgment.

The call to show mercy is the call to live out the gospel. Compared to God, each of us is dirty, smelly, fallen, broken, and incapable of changing our sin-consumed situation. Unchanged, we will suffer his eternal judgment in hell. Yet, in spite of all of our rampant wickedness, God's love motivated him to show mercy to us. Rather than give us what we deserve, he offers us grace and forgiveness. He transforms us into representations of his son and transfers us into his son's glorious kingdom. Then, he calls us to show the same love and authentic mercy to others, who are likewise fallen and broken by sin. As we demonstrate self-control and show God's love to all, regardless of their social status, we reveal the truth of the gospel and the reality of the perfect law of liberty, through which we ourselves receive mercy.

Food for Thought

All of us are drawn towards people who are like us, whether because of ethnicity, education, or social status. Today's text challenges us to understand that God loves everyone equally, and so should we. What about you? How often do you get out of your comfort zone to show God's love to those who are different than you?

Faith in Action

Today, you will be surrounded by people who are different than you but who need to be exposed to God's love. Rather than simply pass them by, look for opportunities to meet a need in their lives. And, consider locating a homeless shelter or community mission in which to serve. If we are not intentional about reaching out to those with the greatest need, we will miss many amazing opportunities to show God's mercy through our lives!

Prayer

As you pray today, spend some time expressing gratitude for all of the amazing ways that God has shown you mercy. Then, talk with God about the things that hold you back on occasion from showing mercy to others. Ask God to expose opportunities for you to pour God's mercy into the lives of others.

James 2:14-19

What good is it, my brothers, if someone says he has faith but does not have works? Can that faith save him? If a brother or sister is poorly clothed and lacking in daily food, and one of you says to them, 'Go in peace, be warmed and filled,' without giving them the things needed for the body, what good is that? So also faith by itself, if it does not have works, is dead. But someone will say, 'You have faith and I have works.' Show me your faith apart from your works, and I will show you my faith by my works. You believe that God is one; you do well. Even the demons believe—and shudder!

In our study of James, we have encountered one overarching theme: obedience is an evidence of authentic faith. In chapter one, we discovered that hearing the word without obeying the word is the worst form of self-deception (1:16, 22, 26). Rather than live this way, however, we are called as Christ-followers to obey God's truth by living with compassion and pursuing justice. This will lead us to embrace and demonstrate authentic mercy.

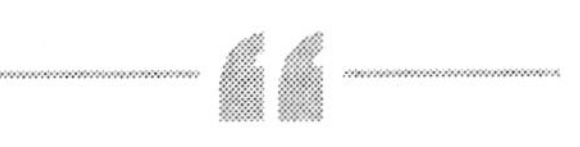

Obedience is an evidence of authentic faith.

With this in mind, James asks a penetrating question: "What good is it, my brothers, if someone says he has faith but does not have works? Can that faith save him?" This text has been the source of much confusion through the years. Clearly, James is not teaching that we can be saved on the basis of works. The New Testament is consistent in its teaching that we receive salvation on the basis of faith alone (Eph 2:8-9). The New Testament is equally clear, however, that authentic faith reveals itself through acts of service (Jn 15:1-11).

We may substitute intention for action. And in doing so, we miss out on the privilege of putting our faith into action for the glory of God.

Following his teaching on how to respond to the poor brother (2:3), it appears that James is challenging the church to show mercy to the poor in tangible ways. Repeatedly, Scripture reveals that food and clothing are the two absolute necessities in life (Mt 6:25-34; 1 Tim 6:6-8). Here, James provides an example of the danger of good intentions. Can you imagine how ridiculous it would be to tell a hungry Christian brother to be well fed without giving him food? Could you imagine telling a freezing Christian sister to be warmed without providing her with a coat? We would never say this out loud to anyone (I hope), but every time we ignore the needs of the poor among us we say it through our actions.

Now, for most of us, this isn't a conscious decision. Many of us are generous to some degree, especially in emergency situations and during the holidays. And, we often intend to do more than we actually attempt. But there is a danger here—we may substitute intention for action. And in doing so, we miss out on the privilege of putting our faith into action for the glory of God.

In verse 17, James makes this sobering statement: "So also faith by itself, if it does not have works, is dead." Any claim of saving faith that does not result in the demonstration of authentic mercy through acts of service is a dead faith—it is devoid of spiritual life.

Any claim of saving faith that does not result in the demonstration of authentic mercy through acts of service is a dead faith.

This is revealed through James' use of the adjective "dead" to describe false faith. We use the same concept in our own speech all the time to refer to things that don't work like they should:

- Dead battery – absence of a charge;
- Dead calm – absence of wind;
- Dead tired – absence of strength;
- Dead end – absence of direction;
- Dead broke – absence of money;
- Dead drunk – absence of sobriety.

Every one of these colloquialisms exists for a reason—they enable us to express that something has totally failed. James did the same thing—he said that faith without works is dead faith. Immediately, we recoil against this statement. How dare James accuse us of having a dead faith simply because we're self-absorbed and sporadic in our devotion!

James is addressing a deeper problem here, however. He is challenging the scores of people who think that belief in God's existence is enough; there is no need for life-change or investment in kingdom labors. To them he offers this advice: "You believe that God is one; you do well. Even the demons believe—and shudder!" Clearly, belief in God's existence is not enough. The most vile, wicked, fallen creatures in the spirit world, the demonic followers of Satan, believe in God's existence. After all, they saw God's glory with their own eyes before they were thrown out of heaven. But they're under God's wrath and destined for hell. So, too, is every person who is separated from God by sin. No amount of belief in God's existence can erase our sin debt. Only a life-transforming encounter with Jesus Christ, through whom we experience forgiveness for our sins, can bring us into true relationship with God. It is in this context that James makes a key statement, "Someone will say, 'You have faith and I have

Any claim of faith that cannot be supported on the basis of an obedient life is dead.

> *Our desire to grow in Christ, even if it is accompanied by occasional failure, is the evidence that we're truly born again.*

works.' Show me your faith apart from your works, and I will show you my faith by my works." Here, James is teaching that there is one thing that gives evidence of authentic life-change: spiritual fruit.

Today, James wants us to understand that it's easy to say we have faith. It's easy to claim that we've been born again. Simply making the claim, however, is not enough. Any claim of faith that cannot be supported on the basis of an obedient life is dead. Remember, James isn't claiming that our works can save us; he is claiming that authentic salvation leads to spiritual works.

Based on what we've learned so far in his book, James would ask:

- Can you claim to have saving faith without the capacity for spiritual endurance?
- Can you claim to have saving faith without the desire to pursue God's wisdom?
- Can you claim to have saving faith without the desire to battle against temptation and sin?
- Can you claim to have saving faith without pursuing self-control in your attitudes and actions?
- Can you claim to have saving faith without hearing and obeying God's truth?
- Can you claim to have saving faith without demonstrating authentic mercy to the poor among us?
- Can you claim to have saving faith without treating all people equally?

Every one of these practical, real life issues help reveal the reality of faith or the absence of faith. Real faith is not attaining sinless perfection. We will not experience that reality until we are in the presence of God in heaven. But, real faith strives daily to grow in all of these areas through the power of the Holy Spirit. Our desire to grow in Christ, even if it is accompanied by occasional failure, is the evidence that we're truly born again. It is the absence of a desire for spiritual things and spiritual fruit that warns us of a lack of saving faith. Faith without works is dead faith. Faith that bears spiritual fruit for the glory of God is saving faith. What kind of faith do you possess?

Food for Thought

Every world religion except for Christianity advocates doing good works in order to earn your salvation. The difference between those religions and Christianity is that Christianity emphasizes a saving relationship with God on the basis of faith in the death and resurrection of Jesus. Today, we were reminded that saving faith is life-changing, and it produces spiritual fruit in our lives. How would you describe your current spiritual growth, specifically as it relates to bearing spiritual fruit in God's kingdom?

Faith in Action

Today, take a minute to read John 15:1-11. As you read it, try to answer these questions: 1) What is the primary evidence that you are connected to Christ? 2) What is the key to bearing much fruit for the glory of God? 3) What is the relationship between bearing fruit and demonstrating that you're a follower of Jesus?

Prayer

As you spend time talking with God today, ask him to continue to grow you in your understanding of how he wants to use you in his kingdom work. If you've become distracted in your spiritual journey, today is the day to renew your commitment to follow Christ and to bear spiritual fruit every day.

James 2:20-26

Do you want to be shown, you foolish person, that faith apart from works is useless? Was not Abraham our father justified by works when he offered up his son Isaac on the altar? You see that faith was active along with his works, and faith was completed by his works; and the Scripture was fulfilled that says, 'Abraham believed God, and it was counted to him as righteousness'—and he was called a friend of God. You see that a person is justified by works and not by faith alone. And in the same way was not also Rahab the prostitute justified by works when she received the messengers and sent them out by another way? For as the body apart from the spirit is dead, so also faith apart from works is dead.

I have several friends who enjoy skydiving. They regularly ask me to accompany them and try it for myself. To this point, I've declined. Of course, it's not that I doubt the safety of the sport. After all, thousands of safe jumps are made every year. I suppose I could say that I have "faith" that all would be well if I jumped out of a plane. In reality, however, my unwillingness to act on my "faith" reveals that I actually have no faith in skydiving at all. Similarly, those who claim to have authentic faith in Christ yet give no evidence of obedience reveal a dead faith as well. In today's text, James is going to continue to develop his argument about the necessity of a faith that works.

To make his point, James is going to use two examples from history. He begins with one of the most significant people in Old Testament history—Abraham, the father of the Jewish nation. In these verses, James mentions the two most significant events in Abraham's life. First, he mentions God's covenant with Abraham. In Genesis 15:1-6, the Bible says that God spoke with Abraham in a vision. In that conversation, God affirmed his promise to bless Abraham. Abraham, in turn, responded with a question—"How can I be blessed when I still don't have an heir?" God's response was simple and clear, "Your very own son shall be your heir. Look toward heaven, and number the stars, if you are able to number them. So shall your offspring be (Gen 15:4-5)." God had been making him this promise for many years, but it had yet to be fulfilled. Abraham and Sarah were growing old. Common sense was screaming that it was too late. This was the moment of truth for Abraham.

In that moment, despite all of the evidence to the contrary, Abraham made the correct decision. For the first time in his life, he placed his faith, his "belief," in the promise of God. And in that moment, God declared him to be righteous. This event is so important to our understanding of the gospel that the apostle Paul devoted all of Romans chapter four to it. In this chapter, Paul emphasizes that Abraham was declared to be righteous by God solely on the basis of faith, before he was circumcised or offered Isaac as a sacrifice. Clearly, Abraham's works had no influence on his conversion.

Yet, as James continues his explanation in today's text, he uses that event as evidence of the fact that Abraham's faith produced spiritual fruit. James wrote, "Was not Abraham our father justified by works when he offered up his son Isaac on the altar? You see that faith was active along with his works, and faith was completed by his works (2:21-22)." Abraham was born again when God declared him to be righteous. In these verses, however, James was emphasizing the reality of Abraham's faith. He demonstrated Abraham's faith by his willingness to obey God's command to offer Isaac as a sacrifice. He trusted

God so much that he believed God could even raise him from the dead if necessary (Heb 11:19). Of course, God never intended to allow Abraham to take Isaac's life, it was simply a test of his faith and obedience. Spiritual fruit is always the evidence of authentic faith. Notice again this key phrase, "You see that faith was active along with his works, and faith was completed by his works." Abraham believed and was justified; then, his life gave evidence of his faith through his obedience to God.

James chose a fascinating Old Testament character for his second example. He wrote, "And in the same way was not also Rahab the prostitute justified by works when she received the messengers and sent them out by another way (2:25)?" To understand this example, we must revisit Rahab's amazing story (Josh 2).

When Joshua led the people into the land of Canaan, Jericho was the first major city he wanted to conquer. In preparation, he sent some spies to explore it. Despite their efforts to remain in the shadows, their presence was soon discovered. As a result, they were forced into hiding as the King's forces began a house-to-house search of the city. As providence would have it, they rushed into the house of a city prostitute named Rahab. While they hid in her house, she managed to convince the soldiers that they had escaped the city, and the soldiers rushed off in pursuit.

Before she helped the men escape by lowering them down the wall from the window of her house, she expressed her simple faith in God. She said, "The LORD your God, he is God in the heavens above and on the earth beneath (Josh 2:11)." She asked the men to show her mercy when Israel attacked her city because she had shown them mercy. They told her to hang a scarlet cord out of her window during the battle and everyone in her house would be spared. That's what she did, and that's exactly what happened.

Spiritual fruit is always the evidence of authentic faith.

Any "faith" that does not give evidence of authenticity through obedience and service is dead faith.

Rahab's incredible faith, which led her to risk her life on behalf of God's people, was affirmed in the great faith chapter of the Bible, Hebrews 11. In verse 31 we read, "By faith Rahab the prostitute did not perish with those who were disobedient, because she had given a friendly welcome to the spies." The writer of Hebrews is affirming that Rahab's faith in God led her to bear the spiritual fruit of hiding the spies. Rahab became a Gentile convert to the God of Israel and is named in the lineage of Jesus (Mt 1:5).

After citing Abraham and Rahab as beautiful examples of authentic faith that produces spiritual fruit, James concludes this section with these words, "For as the body apart from the spirit is dead, so also faith apart from works is dead." Everything James wrote following 2:14 has been building to this statement. There is no room for debate here. James is not prepared to allow a cheap understanding of the gospel to creep into the church. He will not allow those who "believe" in God's existence to go comfortably into hell. Any "faith" that does not give evidence of authenticity through obedience and service is dead faith. Only faith in Jesus Christ's death and resurrection, accompanied by a life that bears fruit for the glory of God, is living faith!

Food for Thought

Abraham and Rahab placed their faith in God in unique circumstances. Both of them demonstrated their faith through their actions. Abraham obeyed by risking his future, and Rahab obeyed by risking her life. There is a theme here. Authentic faith leads to the kind of obedience that embraces risk to serve God and others. As a follower of Jesus, how would you describe your ministry service? When was the last time you took a risk in kingdom life? Honestly, every act of service involves some risk, because we have to get out of our comfort zone to serve God. Is God leading you to take a risk for him? If so, what is it?

Faith in Action

For the last two days we've been thinking about the way in which authentic faith produces spiritual fruit. Call your church this week to inquire about ministry opportunities that are currently available, including those that minister to the poor in your community. Consider going on a mission trip in your own area or internationally. Look for new opportunities this week to demonstrate authentic faith through service.

Prayer

In your prayer time today, ask God to deepen your desire to bear fruit. Ask him for the courage to take risks by getting out of your comfort zone as you follow him in obedience.

James 3:1-8

Not many of you should become teachers, my brothers, for you know that we who teach will be judged with greater strictness. For we all stumble in many ways. And if anyone does not stumble in what he says, he is a perfect man, able also to bridle his whole body. If we put bits into the mouths of horses so that they obey us, we guide their whole bodies as well. Look at the ships also: though they are so large and are driven by strong winds, they are guided by a very small rudder wherever the will of the pilot directs. So also the tongue is a small member, yet it boasts of great things. How great a forest is set ablaze by such a small fire! And the tongue is a fire, a world of unrighteousness. The tongue is set among our members, staining the whole body, setting on fire the entire course of life, and set on fire by hell. For every kind of beast and bird, of reptile and sea creature, can be tamed and has been tamed by mankind, but no human being can tame the tongue. It is a restless evil, full of deadly poison.

Words are powerful things, and like glue, they stick to you for life. I learned this lesson very early. When I was in the fifth grade, I had the most amazing teacher—Mr. Booth. I suppose he made such an impression on me because he was the only male teacher I had in elementary school. He was the picture of everything I aspired to be—he was smart, strong, athletic, and handsome. He also coached all of the elementary boy's teams. So, when he spoke, I listened.

One day he was sitting beside me on a playground bench. Out of nowhere he said, "Billy, are you waiting on a flood?" I had never been asked such a question, and so I had no idea how to reply. He told me to stand up. Then he said, "Look down at your pants." I gazed at my feet as he continued. "Look how high those things are. Why, we could have 6" of floodwater and those britches wouldn't even get wet."

I didn't know exactly why, but suddenly I felt awkward and embarrassed. My hero had just mocked me—or so I thought. He looked me in the eye and asked me a profound question for a fifth grade boy. "Do you ever want to have a girlfriend?" Now I was really embarrassed, but I nodded the affirmative. "Then you're going to have to do something about those pants." With that, he walked away. You can bet I had my mom get me some new pants that very day, and soon Julie, the prettiest girl in the sixth grade, was my special friend. I loved Mr. Booth

While this is a silly story, it reflects the profound impact that words can have on us, in both a positive and negative way. After all, I still remember this conversation like it was yesterday. I remember other conversations from throughout my life as well, and many of them are far more painful than this one. I imagine you can relate.

In chapter three, James challenges his readers to live a legacy of godly communication. He begins by challenging the godly men in his church who aspire to leadership to understand what's required of them—they must reject godless speech. James has already challenged the entire church about this issue (1:26), but he is going to expand upon it in today's text. The primary reason James gives for this warning is that God will judge those with authority in his church with "greater strictness." It is a warning that all church Elders should understand.

Nevertheless, what is good for the Elders of a church is good for everyone in the church, so James is going to challenge each of us to examine the way we communicate with those around us. This whole text is summed up in one phrase: "The tongue is a fire." James is using the word "tongue" as a substitute for speech, because speech is impossible without the tongue. To make his point, he uses the common metaphor of fire. Fire can be used for great good. For instance, we have a large, wood-burning fireplace in our home, and I build a fire on almost every winter day. The warmth and beauty of a fire is a source of great comfort to me. But, fire can also have devastating consequences. When it is out of control, it destroys everything in its path—forests, homes, and lives.

Similarly, our speech can be used to provide either comfort or devastation. In this text, James reminds us that we all have the potential to sin greatly through our speech. In fact, he uses several strong descriptions to drive home this point. He says the tongue is "a world of unrighteousness." Left unchecked, our words can contain filth, anger, and hate—the very opposite of God's intention. Next, he says that the tongue "stains the whole body." Unrighteous language makes us spiritually dirty. Literally, this means our verbal excrement stains us. Then, James says that the tongue "sets our life on fire." Like a fire, unrighteous speech has the potential to destroy the lives of those around us, and to destroy our own lives as a result. Again, he says that the tongue is "set on fire by hell." In other words, our filthy, angry, hate-filled speech pleases Satan but breaks our Father's heart. James continues by saying the tongue is "untamable." It is like a wild stallion; it cannot be broken until it is captured. Finally, he says the tongue is a "restless evil, full of deadly poison." Language is restless—we use it all day, every day. Sadly, unrighteous language produces audible venom, and like that of a rattlesnake, its bite is both quick and deadly.

> *Ungodly language produces audible venom, and like that of a rattlesnake, its bite is both quick and deadly.*

James teaches us that we can all fall into the trap of ungodly speech. Occasional ungodly speech reveals that our hearts are resisting God, and we are in need

The Holy Spirit alone can contain and control our speech.

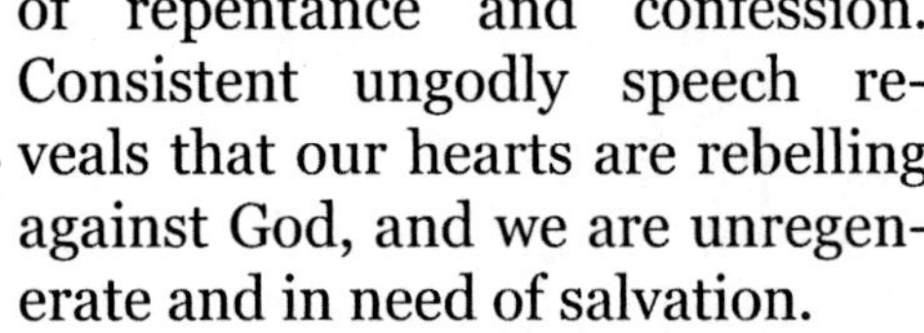

of repentance and confession. Consistent ungodly speech reveals that our hearts are rebelling against God, and we are unregenerate and in need of salvation.

As followers of Christ, we face a daily battle with our own speech. Yet, our speech is a gift from God. We can speak because we are made in his image. Similarly, speech can be a gift to others, if the Holy Spirit controls it. The Spirit is the bit in the horse's mouth and the rudder of the ship. He alone can contain and control our speech. Every day we must submit control of our speech to God.

Ephesians 4:29 provides us with great truth about how to do this. It says, "Let no corrupting talk come out of your mouths, but only such as is good for building up, as fits the occasion, that it may give grace to those who hear." We should train ourselves to ask these questions about our speech:

1. Will my words build up or tear down the person to whom I'm speaking? I can speak edifying words that delight or corrupting words that demean—the choice is mine. My words can be affirming even if they convey difficult information.
2. Will my words benefit or burden the person to whom I'm speaking? Our conversations always occur in a particular context. Sometimes it is a positive context and sometimes it is a negative context. But in every context we have control over how we say what we need to say. Generally, words that build are words that benefit, while words that tear down are words that place a heavy burden upon the person to whom we are speaking.
3. Will my words help or hurt the person to whom I'm speaking? This is the ultimate test of all of

our communication—does it give grace. In other words, does it reveal that we love and respect the person to whom we're speaking as one who is made in God's image. Honestly, you can give grace regardless of the content of the conversation, if you are intentional about building and benefiting the person to whom you are speaking.

Today, on average, we will speak some 15,000-25,000 words. May God the Holy Spirit empower us to use words that build, benefit, and bless the ones to whom we speak.

Food for Thought

You will speak to many people today—family, friends, colleagues, and even strangers. You will talk with them about both serious and silly things. How will their lives be different because they spent time talking to you? Will they leave encouraged because they spoke to you or will their load be a little heavier? Consider the ways you can bless those you speak to today.

Faith in Action

As an exercise today, put a rubber band around your wrist to remind you that you are connected to the people around you in some pretty important ways. Every time you feel or see that rubber band, let it remind you to see each conversation as an opportunity to bless the people around you.

Prayer

As you pray, remember that God is another person that you have the opportunity to talk with every day. You can bless God as you praise him in your prayers. Ask him to help you find ways to encourage the people you speak with today.

James 3:9-16

With it we bless our Lord and Father, and with it we curse people who are made in the likeness of God. From the same mouth come blessing and cursing. My brothers, these things ought not to be so. Does a spring pour forth from the same opening both fresh and salt water? Can a fig tree, my brothers, bear olives, or a grapevine produce figs? Neither can a salt pond yield fresh water. Who is wise and understanding among you? By his good conduct let him show his works in the meekness of wisdom. But if you have bitter jealousy and selfish ambition in your hearts, do not boast and be false to the truth. This is not the wisdom that comes down from above, but is earthly, unspiritual, demonic. For where jealousy and selfish ambition exist, there will be disorder and every vile practice. But the wisdom from above is first pure, then peaceable, gentle, open to reason, full of mercy and good fruits, impartial and sincere. And a harvest of righteousness is sown in peace by those who make peace.

An interesting phrase developed in America during the years leading up to the American Revolution. It goes like this: "You speak with a forked tongue." While you have probably heard this phrase, you may not know its etymology. Snakes are creatures that most hold in disdain. Interestingly, their tongues are split at the end and filled with scent receptors, which help them to smell and trail potential prey (gross, right?). Native American Indians were the first to use this physical trait of snakes to describe people. It was a phrase that meant to speak out of both sides of

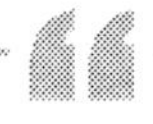

Some things don't go together or grow together. In this case, it's believers and hateful speech.

your mouth; to say one thing and mean another; or to say one thing to one person and something different to another person, based solely on the need of the moment. Over time, it has become one of most common North American metaphors for describing the person whose words cannot be trusted.

James makes the same claim in today's passage. He says that with the tongue "we bless our Lord and Father, and with it we curse people who are made in the likeness of God. From the same mouth come blessing and cursing (3:9-10)." In other words, he tells us that we all have a tendency to speak with a forked tongue. We have no trouble praising God in worship or our personal devotions, but we also have no trouble cursing people who make us angry or frustrated. Yet, they're image-bearers of God, just like us. We're to reveal our authentic religion by making them recipients of grace (1:26-27). We're to love them without impartiality, because they're our neighbors (2:8-9). We're to demonstrate our living faith through our gracious words (2:18). Instead, however, we may demonstrate just the opposite through our use of hateful speech. James is correct when he says, "My brothers, these things ought not to be so."

To prove his point, James uses some great examples from nature. He asks, "Does a spring pour forth from the same opening both fresh and salt water? Can a fig tree, my brothers, bear olives, or a grapevine produce figs? Neither can a salt pond yield fresh water." James teaching is obvious—some things don't go together or grow together. In this case, it's believers and hateful speech.

So, what are we supposed to do with this truth? James says, "Who is wise and understanding among you? By his good conduct let him show his works in the meekness of wisdom." This reminds us of what he says in 1:5-8. The way we use our tongue gives evidence to the existence of wisdom in our lives—or not. Ultimately, our conduct reveals if we are wise, because it reflects the degree to which we accept and obey God's truth for how to live our lives. Perhaps nowhere is this more clearly seen than in the way we use our speech. In the concluding verses of today's text, James is going to describe a couple of sinful emotions and motives that have the potential to capture our hearts. And when they do, wicked speech will be on display too.

The phrase "bitter jealousy" refers to an emotion. It's the emotion we may feel when someone we know experiences a success that we wish was our own. We may feel it towards the guy who gets the promotion or the lady who gets the great guy. The questions begin to roll around in our heads. Why didn't I get that promotion? Why did she get that guy? How is he better than me? What does she have that I don't? Left unchecked, this bitter root will produce some hateful fruit in our lives. Soon, we'll be directing our anger against him, or her, through our speech. We may slander him, or mock her, as a means of soothing our own burning emotions. Yet, we're the ones who are hurt in the end—along with our testimonies. Rather than trusting God to fulfill his purpose in our lives, even when things don't happen as we'd like, we fume about the things that might have been.

The phrase "selfish ambition" literally means to "politic" for an office. It was used primarily of secular politicians working towards election, but James notes that it can also refer to people who are trying to obtain positions of influence in a local church. At its core, this phrase means to "put oneself forward" at the expense of others. Clearly, this motive is based on "arrogance," because we have an overinflated sense of our own worth and abilities.

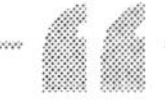

There is a fine line between the desire to succeed and being driven to succeed.

James 3:9-16

Ambition is a dangerous master. After all, there is a fine line between the desire to succeed and being driven to succeed. The first may be an evidence of doing your best for the glory of God. The second may be an evidence of doing your best for the glory of you. The first is based upon a proper understanding of accountability; the second is based upon the selfish desires for personal achievement.

James teaches us that bitter jealousy and selfish ambition are not fruits of the Spirit. Rather, they are "earthly, natural, demonic." While we may be able to hide these sinful emotions and motives for a while, eventually our speech will reveal them. James says that where these things exist, there is "disorder and every vile practice." In other words, there is the potential for destructive actions and devastating words.

Today, you will have numerous opportunities to demonstrate that God's wisdom is at work in your life. First, you may face circumstances that may tempt you to be jealous. How will you respond? Will you resort to the use of bitter, angry thoughts and words, or will you trust in God's purpose for your life? Second, you may face circumstances that tempt you to be selfishly ambitious. Will you push yourself ahead, or over, someone else in your pursuit of a goal? Will you attempt to harm someone by speaking ill of him or her, or will you work hard and trust God with the outcome? Third, you may face circumstances that tempt you to use the kind of speech that is the furthest thing from God's heart. Will you let anger control you and your words, or will you let the Holy Spirit control you and provide you with words of grace? Today is a new day—live it for God's glory!

Food for Thought

Our motives are the hardest things for us to honestly assess. Spend some time today thinking about your life. Are you jealous of someone? Who is it? Is that jealousy making you bitter towards life and God? What about your goals? Are they surrendered to God's will or are you doing everything in your power to make them happen—no matter who gets hurt? How are these sinful motives affecting your speech? Is it characterized by grace or hate?

Faith in Action

Today, you will have an opportunity to think differently about jealousy and selfish ambition. Write 1 Cor 10:31 on a note card and keep it with you today. Read this verse every time you are tempted to be jealous or selfish. Allow it to remind you that you have one goal— to live for God's glory. You will be amazed at how this will guard your heart from sinful motives and speech.

Prayer

If you find that your heart is being affected by sinful motives, which lead to sinful actions and speech, spend time in prayer today talking with God about it. Ask God for forgiveness and commit to trust him in these areas of your life.

James 3:17-18

But the wisdom from above is first pure, then peaceable, gentle, open to reason, full of mercy and good fruits, impartial and sincere. And a harvest of righteousness is sown in peace by those who make peace.

There are few things in life more unsettling than a fractured relationship. Like a fractured bone, it is painful. Sadly, these breaks are often self-inflicted. Each of us has the potential to damage a relationship with every word we speak and with every action we take. Consequently, it is easy to understand why our relationships often suffer as a result.

James concludes his discourse on the danger of sinful speech, and the havoc it creates, by providing us with a remedy. Interestingly, he links it back to one of his first admonitions: "If any of you lacks wisdom, let him ask God, who gives generously to all without reproach, and it will be given him (1:5)." James states what we all instinctively know—we need God's wisdom in our lives. Perhaps nowhere is this truer than when it comes to our emotions, and the speech and actions they produce.

Yesterday, we observed what the absence of God's wisdom from our lives looks like—it is "earthly, unspiritual, demonic (3:15)." Today's text reveals what the presence of God's wisdom looks like in our lives. James provides a list that describes God's wisdom. First, God's wisdom is pure. This word means to be unsoiled. It is the opposite of "evil" (3:8). Purity is an expression of holiness, one of

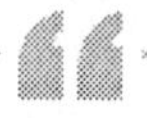

We need God's wisdom in our lives. Perhaps nowhere is this truer than when it comes to our emotions, and the speech and actions they produce.

God's primary characteristics. In Scripture, believers are repeatedly admonished to pursue holiness and to think about things that are pure (Phil 4:8). The wisdom that God gives is rooted in holiness of thought and action.

Second, God's wisdom is peaceable. This word is interesting. It means to be free from chaos or confusion. Chaos results from an undisciplined life, and it is often accompanied by "restless" lips (3:8). Few things can create more chaos than undisciplined speech. Instead, God has saved us to be people of peace (Mt 5:9). The wisdom that God gives produces peace with him and others.

Third, God's wisdom is gentle. This word is challenging to translate into English. Literally, it means to "meet in the middle." It is a word that is used to describe a willingness to compromise. Of course, the Bible never uses this word to mean that compromise concerning sin is acceptable. Rather, it acknowledges that we do not possess absolute knowledge—only God does. That's why we need his wisdom in every situation (Pr 18:17). The wisdom that God gives warns against stubborn dogmatism.

Fourth, God's wisdom is open to reason. This word means to be capable of being persuaded. It is a companion word to "gentle." God's wisdom, which teaches us to meet in the middle when we are faced with relational issues, requires us to be open to the wisdom of others. If we're unwilling to meet someone in the middle, we will never be open to being persuaded in regards to the important decisions we must make. This is especially true when we are having these discussions with other believers. If we're all seeking God's wisdom, and we meet in the middle with humble spirits, we will be mutually persuaded as to the best course of action. The wisdom that God gives encourages us to embrace humility rather than hubris.

Fifth, God's wisdom is full of mercy and good fruits. This phrase means to be "stuffed" with a compassion that produces acts of love towards others. This is the way that God treats us. Despite our sin, God continues to shower us with new mercy every day (Lam 3:22-23). Consequently, he wants us to treat others in the same way.

If we choose wrongly the "earthly, unspiritual, demonic" path, we will be motivated by jealousy and selfish ambition (3:14). Consequently, we will steamroll anyone in our path in the attempt to have our way. However, when God's wisdom is shaping our thoughts and actions, we will value the contributions of others to the conversations of our lives, and we will treat them in a way that reveals that we value them.

Sixth, God's wisdom is impartial. In other words, it is free from favoritism. Remember James' teaching in 2:1-9? James summarized his teaching there with this statement: "If you show partiality, you are committing sin and are convicted by the law as transgressors." Ouch! Favoritism can be a dangerous foe of wisdom. It is dangerous because it may convince us to listen to the wrong voices when facing important decisions. Rather than seeking the wise counsel of godly people, we may choose the counsel of famous secularists, which is always a bad decision. Instead, James challenges us to understand that God may reveal his wisdom in unlikely ways using unlikely people. Further, if we're in a position of authority, we must seek to lead in a way that gives equal value and opportunity to all people.

> *"When God's wisdom is shaping our thoughts and actions, we will value the contributions of others to the conversations of our lives, and we will treat them in a way that reveals that we value them."*

Seventh, and finally, God's wisdom is sincere. This word means without hypocrisy. It is a word that speaks to the authenticity of a person's relationship with

Ultimately, our lives and speech will reveal whether we are embracing God's wisdom or following our own foolish agendas.

God. In 3:14, James said that those who are driven by bitter jealousy and selfish ambition are "false to the truth." In other words, they're hypocrites. They say one thing with their lips, but their hearts and actions reveal something different. Those who are seeking God's wisdom are characterized by sincerity. Does this mean that they're sinless? No. They are fully aware of their potential to be trapped by pride. As a result, they live each day seeking and trusting in God's wisdom. They are honest about their own trouble spots, which makes them willing to believe and trust God for the wisdom to avoid them.

James provides us with seven beautiful descriptions of God's wisdom. But why does God extend the offer of this wisdom to us? James gives us the answer: "And a harvest of righteousness is sown in peace by those who make peace." This is farming language. If you want a good harvest, you've got to sow good seed into good soil. The same is true in our relationships. If you want a harvest of righteousness, you must sow peace into your relationships.

How is this done? Not by jealousy and selfish ambition. Those selfish traits produce "disorder and every vile practice (3:16)." God's wisdom is the antidote to this problem. We are sowing peace into our relationships when we infuse them with purity, peace, gentleness, reason, mercy and good fruits, impartiality, and sincerity.

James wrote these words in 3:13: "Who is wise and understanding among you? By his good conduct let him show his works in the meekness of wisdom." Ultimately, our lives and speech will reveal whether we are embracing God's wisdom or following our own foolish agendas. In the Bible, the word "meekness" does not mean "weakness." Instead, it means "power under control." It was used to refer to the way in which horses are controlled by the use of a bit (3:3). In the same way, God's wisdom has the potential to control our thoughts, motives, and actions. Left to ourselves, we will make a mess of any situation. Yet, if we embrace God's wisdom, our choices will bring health and peace into our relationships.

Food for Thought

Think about all of the relationships you have. You have relationships with your family, your friends, your co-workers, your neighbors, the people you meet socially, and the people in your church. Some of these people you interact with regularly, while others you may only see on occasion. Yet, each of these relationships has unique characteristics. How can God's wisdom sow peace into each of these relationships?

Faith in Action

You will face the potential for conflict in your relationships today. You may have a disagreement with a co-worker, your spouse, or the coach of your child's little league team. When you are faced with the decision about how to respond, pause to consider how applying God's wisdom to the situation would produce peace rather than disorder. You will be amazed how applying these seven wisdom principles will restore harmony to a relationship! To do this, however, you must be able to remember these principles. So, take the time to memorize James 3:17-18 today.

Prayer

Today, ask God again for wisdom (1:5). In fact, you may need to ask him for wisdom many times today! Specifically, ask God to help you apply these wisdom principles in your relationships today.

James 4:1-6

What causes quarrels and what causes fights among you? Is it not this, that your passions are at war within you? You desire and do not have, so you murder. You covet and cannot obtain, so you fight and quarrel. You do not have, because you do not ask. You ask and do not receive, because you ask wrongly, to spend it on your passions. You adulterous people! Do you not know that friendship with the world is enmity with God? Therefore whoever wishes to be a friend of the world makes himself an enemy of God. Or do you suppose it is to no purpose that the Scripture says, "He yearns jealously over the spirit that he has made to dwell in us?" But he gives more grace. Therefore it says, "God opposes the proud, but gives grace to the humble."

People fight over the craziest things. When I was a policeman I watched people fight over kids, property, and money. Once I responded to a crime scene where a guy had been murdered over a cigarette! The desire for things is strong in each of us. It may tempt us to cut corners in our pursuit of them or to become jealous of others who have more than us. Left unchecked, it can quickly consume our lives.

In today's text, James examines the ultimate source of the "jealousy and selfish ambition" that produces "disorder and every vile practice" in so many areas of our lives (3:14-16). He asks this question: "What causes quarrels and what causes fights among you? Is it not this, that your passions are at war within you?" The word that is

Pride is the root cause of every sin, including the sin of discontentment and the coveting it produces.

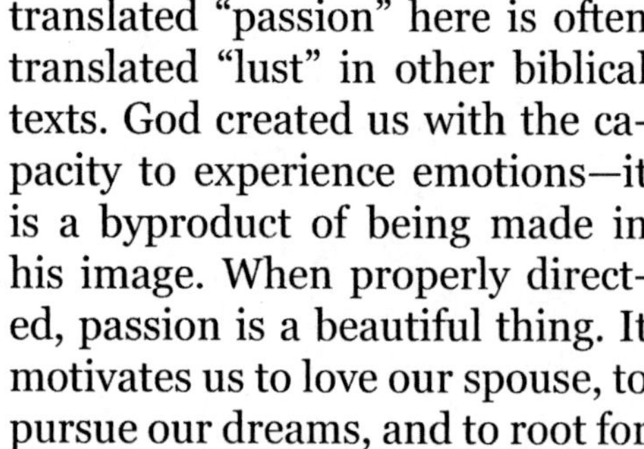

translated "passion" here is often translated "lust" in other biblical texts. God created us with the capacity to experience emotions—it is a byproduct of being made in his image. When properly directed, passion is a beautiful thing. It motivates us to love our spouse, to pursue our dreams, and to root for our favorite college football team. When improperly directed, however, it can become a source of every type of evil. Literally, this word means "passion that is out of control," and it refers to an overdose of personal desire.

Because selfishness is our sinful default setting, we are prone to view every situation on the basis of how it affects us personally. And, if we're not seeking to know and live God's wisdom (3:17-18), we are likely to choose a self-focused response. James identifies two specific ways that this happens. First, we turn our personal goals into idols. He writes, "You desire and do not have, so you murder." Clearly, James is using the word "murder" as figurative language—they weren't literally killing each other. But, because of their sinful passion to achieve their goals, they were willing to climb on or over anyone who stood in the way.

Second, we turn the personal successes of others into idols. James continues, "You covet and cannot obtain, so you fight and quarrel." Here, "covet" means to crave what belongs to others. It is always the result of discontentment. When some of the people in James' church saw the financial resources or abilities of others, things they couldn't obtain for themselves, it made them jealous and bitter. As a result, they routinely complained about their circumstances.

The pursuit of these idols even affected their prayers. James says, "You do not have, because you do not ask. You ask and do not receive, because you ask wrongly, to spend it on your passions." Notice, these people were praying! They were involved in religious activity, but they weren't receiving anything from God. Why? God knew their hearts. They weren't asking for financial blessings in order that they might bless others; they were asking for those blessings so that they could obtain the status and possessions that had become their idols.

James continues by identifying the underlying heart problem that was leading to their selfish discontent: they had disloyal hearts. James calls them "adulterous people." Rather than trust God and live with contentment, they maintained a love affair with the world. They fully embraced its definitions of success and personal value. They honestly believed that the secret to happiness in life was found through possessions and position. They had chosen friendship with the world without realizing that they had become enemies of God. There is huge irony here. God alone could provide everything they wanted. Yet, rather than submit to his will and seek his favor, they were trying to make their success happen through their own feeble efforts.

Ultimately, of course, the real culprit here is pride. Pride is the root cause of every sin, including the sin of discontentment and the coveting it produces. Here's the thing about pride—God hates it! James writes, "God opposes the proud." The word "oppose" is an interesting one. It means to "stand against." It was a word used to describe an army standing like an immovable object before invaders. God stands against pride every time he sees it, even in the lives of his kids.

Pride, at its core, is the belief that our will and desires for our lives are more important than God's will and desire for our lives. If we yield to pride, it is because we have yet to believe that God's plans are best for us (Jer 29:11). As a result, we will live with divided loyalties. We will hold on to God with one hand and hold on

Pride is the belief that our will and desires for our lives are more important than God's will and desire for our lives.

God wants us to live in humility rather than live with a pride-filled heart.

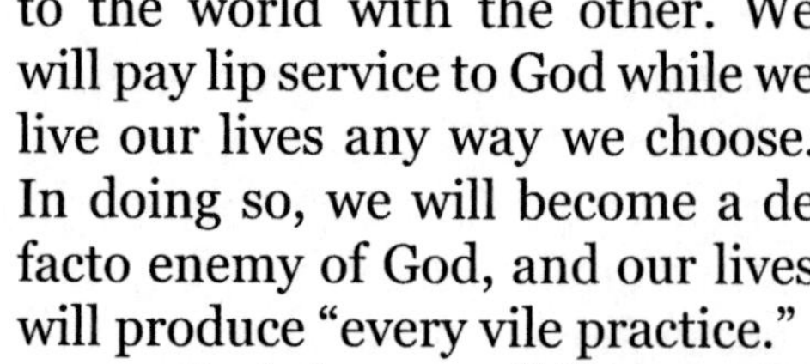

to the world with the other. We will pay lip service to God while we live our lives any way we choose. In doing so, we will become a de facto enemy of God, and our lives will produce "every vile practice."

God has a different desire for us, however. He wants to pour his grace and provision into our lives. James concludes, "He gives more grace. . . . [he] gives grace to the humble." God wants us to live in humility rather than live with a pride-filled heart. Humility is the ability to see God as he is, and as a result, to see ourselves as we are. We are finite, sinful people who are susceptible to pride and its crushing effects. God is infinite, holy, and wise. He is sovereign over his creation and our lives. God promises to give us his grace and wisdom, so that we may walk with him and others in humility. And, he promises to fill our lives and relationships with joy and peace if we will simply follow him.

Food for Thought

Are you struggling with discontentment in some area of your life today? If so, it's important to understand that it's is a dangerous enemy. Here is the progression that discontentment follows as it grows in your life. First, you experience an unmet expectation in your life. For instance, you don't get the raise you were anticipating at work. This can become a seed of discontentment. Second, you make an appeal for resolution. You meet with your boss, share your concern, and ask him for the raise. Third, you are unwilling to accept the resolution. You went to your boss about your raise, and he told you that the company decided not to give you the raise based upon your recent performance. At this point, you have a decision to make. You can choose to accept your boss' explanation, or you can become angrier about this financial slight. Fourth, you become bitter and discontent. If you choose anger over resolution, you will become increasingly bitter at work. This is the point at which the seed of discontentment begins to bear fruit in your life. Fifth, you begin to blame others rather than engage in some self-assessment. In reality, you may not deserve the raise. But, rather than even ask yourself if there are some areas where you can improve, you begin to blame everyone else for your lack of a raise. You may blame your co-workers, or your manager, or your boss. This only deepens your sense of discontentment. Sixth, and finally, you find others with whom to share your misery. It's been said, "misery loves company." If discontentment consumes your heart at work, you will soon be hanging out with all of the other people who are motivated by discontentment. Today, pause to reflect on your job, your marriage, your church, and your life as a whole. Are you somewhere on this descending journey into discontentment? If so, today would be a great day to confess that sin and begin to be content with God's sovereign work in your life.

Faith in Action

Today, you may be tempted by discontentment. It could appear in the most unlikely ways. Should it happen, try responding with this strategy. If you are tempted to be disappointed because you have failed to achieve a goal, or if you are tempted to be jealous of someone else who has, focus on a positive in your life instead. For instance, if you're frustrated that you're not making the grades you'd like, focus on being grateful for the opportunity to be in school. If you're struggling with a problem at work, focus on being grateful that you have a job. If you're disappointed in your spouse for some reason, make a list of the things that you appreciate about him or her. You will be amazed at how turning a negative into a positive will protect you from misplaced passions!

Prayer

Contentment is critical for success in our lives as believers. Today, spend time thanking God for his blessings in your life. Be specific—call those blessings out by name. Then, ask God to help you live with an attitude of gratitude today!

James 4:7-10

Submit yourselves therefore to God. Resist the Devil, and he will flee from you. Draw near to God, and he will draw near to you. Cleanse your hands, you sinners, and purify your hearts, you double-minded. Be wretched and mourn and weep. Let your laughter be turned to mourning and your joy to gloom. Humble yourselves before the Lord, and he will exalt you.

It's one thing to know that something needs to change; it's another thing altogether to know how to change it. Several years ago I took over the responsibility for managing our family finances. My wife had done an excellent job, but she was ready for a break. When I began, I was totally overwhelmed. I had never done it before, and I wasn't even sure where to begin. I knew that I needed to change my understanding about personal finances, so I dove into the process. I read some great books on developing and managing a budget, sought some counsel from my buddies, and began. The results were amazing. I was able to see firsthand how wise stewardship produces financial stability and success. Also, I was growing as our family's shepherd. All of this happened because I knew that something needed to change, and I was willing to do whatever it took to make that change happen.

In today's text, James continues to develop the topic he began in 3:13. He is contrasting two polar opposites: pride and humility. As we've seen already, pride is rebellion against God and his will. Its primary manifestation is our lives is selfishness, which readily embraces lust, coveting,

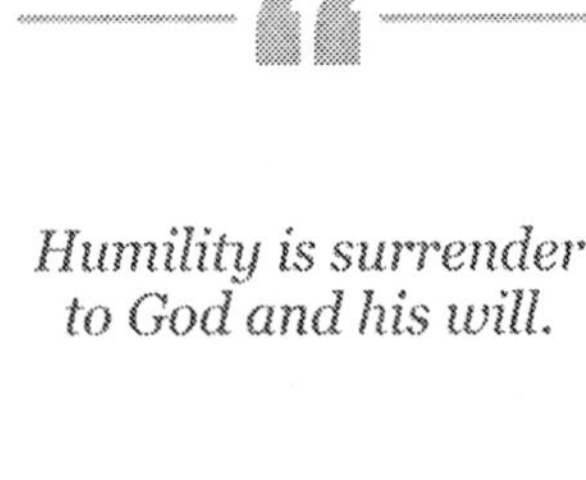

jealousy, slander, discontentment, and a host of other sins. It begins in the heart, but it soon spills out on to every relationship we have. It produces conflicts, fighting, bitter envy, self-promotion, and self-preservation. It is unspiritual, and it is the enemy of peace in our relationships—with both God and others.

Humility, on the other hand, is surrender to God and his will. It readily embraces God's word and wisdom for life. Its primary manifestation is selflessness, which reveals itself through self-control, edifying words, a spirit of contentment, and authentic devotion to God. It, too, begins in the heart and has a profound influence on our relationships. It produces relational harmony, because it is "pure, peaceable, gentle, open to reason, full of mercy and good fruits, impartial and sincere (3:17)." It is spiritual, and it produces peace in our relationships—with both God and others.

Let's be honest. Our lives are more likely to be characterized by pride than by humility. Oh sure, we may talk about the value and need for humility in our lives, but we are expert practitioners of pride. After all, most of us have had years of practice rebelling against God and his will. Yet, as we saw yesterday, "God opposes the proud, but gives grace to the humble (4:6)." None of us want God to "stand against" us because of our pride. As a result, the cultivation of humility in our hearts and lives is a must!

The question is this: How in the world do we do it? Thankfully, James gives us the answer in today's text. He identifies four steps that we can take every day to cultivate humility in our hearts. The first step we must take every day is to submit ourselves to God. The word "submit" means to "place oneself under another." This means that we are choosing to place ourselves under God's authority on a daily basis, rather than relating to him as an enemy

(4:4). For this to occur, we must make two conscious decisions.

Decision 1: Resist the Devil. "Resist," here, means to "stand against" Satan. It's the same word used to describe how God stands against the proud. We, too, must stand against pride and its evil manifestations in our lives. We must live with an understanding that Satan makes it his business to destroy people, and he would love to do the same to us (1 Pet 5:8). God makes us a promise here: When we resist Satan's temptation to live with a pride-filled heart, he will move on to other potential victims.

Decision 2: Draw near to God. We are always either moving closer to God or moving further away from him—we are never static. Every day we must choose to move towards him. He wants to pour grace and blessing into our lives, and he will if we submit in humility to his will and word (4:6). God makes us another promise here: When we draw near to him, he draws near to us! God may stand against the proud, but he loves to hang out with the humble. It is amazing to know that we can live in close fellowship with God every day!

The second step we must take every day is to practice daily confession for our sins. Specifically, James is referencing the particular sins of the people in his church (4:1-4). Certainly, we are capable of those very same sins on a daily basis. However, submission to God serves as an antidote to many prideful sins. When we do sin, however, we must practice confession (1 Jn 1:9). This involves two specific prayers: The first prayer is this: "Forgive our sin." This refers to sins of commission—sins that "dirty our hands" daily, like anger, selfishness, and an untamed tongue (3:6). When we commit these sins, we must submit our hearts to God quickly through confession (we may need to confess our sins to those we have wronged, too).

The cultivation of humility in our hearts and lives is a must!

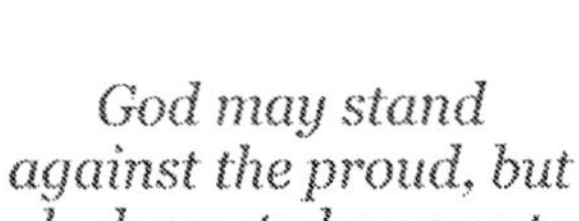

God may stand against the proud, but he loves to hang out with the humble.

The second prayer is this: "Focus our minds." This refers specifically to the sin of pride. James writes, "Purify your hearts, you double-minded." He began his book by telling us that a "double-minded man is unstable in all his ways (1:8)." We are double-minded when we try to serve God and the Devil at the same time. Jesus tells us that this is impossible. "No one can serve two masters, for either he will hate the one and love the other, or he will be devoted to one and despise the other (Mt 6:24)." While Jesus was talking specifically about the decision to serve either God or our money, the principle is true in this context as well—you cannot serve God through humility, while at the same time serving Satan through pride. When we succumb to pride, we must confess that sin to God immediately; then, we must ask for his aid in focusing our minds on his will and word through humility.

The third step we must take every day is to cultivate godly sorrow and repentance in our hearts. James continues, "Be wretched and mourn and weep. Let your laughter be turned to mourning and your joy to gloom." He isn't advocating that we live a life of consistent doom and gloom. That would be in opposition to many of God's commands (Ps 118:24). He is challenging us to cultivate godly sorrow over our sin, however. The reality is that we're so used to living in a sinful world that we fail to remember that God hates sin. He hates it because it marred his good creation and required his Son to die on the cross in order to atone for it. As a result, we must learn to hate its presence in our own hearts too. That is what real repentance is—the ability to mourn over our sins and to turn away from them.

The fourth step we must take every day is to fully embrace the call to humility. After all, Jesus is the perfect example of humility (Phil 2:5-11), and God wants us to become like him. There is spiritual irony here. Satan tempts us to believe that we can have everything we want if we'll just do whatever it takes to obtain it. In actuality, the opposite is true. God is the source of every blessing, and he pours them out on those who submit to him through humility. James concludes, "Humble yourselves before the Lord, and he will exalt you."

God is the source of every blessing, and he pours them out on those who submit to him through humility.

Food for Thought

If you're like me, your to-do list is packed today. Your performance of the tasks that lie before you will impact your success in many ways, not only today but also in the future. There are only two ways to approach this day. The first way is to do it alone. You can plan your day, call the shots, and try to force your way to the success you crave. This is the path of pride. The second way is to do it with God. You can plan your day, submit your plans to God, work your plan, and trust God with the outcomes. This is the path of humility, and it is the path that leads to God's favor in your life.

Faith in Action

It is easy to begin the day with a surrendered heart, only to slip back into self-mode as the day progresses. Today, write the words "Who are you serving?" on a post-it note and put it someplace where you will see it often. It will remind you to walk in humility—even when the pressure is on!

Prayer

As you talk with God today, work through the four steps he has given you to help develop humility in your heart (submit to God; practice daily confession; cultivate godly sorrow and repentance for sin; embrace humility). As needed, spend time talking with him about each area. Then, commit your to-do list to him, and ask for his favor as you follow him.

James 4:11-12

Do not speak evil against one another, brothers. The one who speaks against a brother or judges his brother, speaks evil against the law and judges the law. But if you judge the law, you are not a doer of the law, but a judge. There is only one lawgiver and judge, he who is able to save and destroy. But who are you to judge your neighbor?

The word "Pharisee" has a very negative connotation in our vocabulary. In fact, it has become synonymous with a hypocritical and judgmental spirit. In Jesus' day, the Pharisees epitomized these traits. They had created a system of rules in an attempt to protect the people from breaking the 10 commandments. Of course, the people struggled to obey them, and the Pharisees were experts at judging them for their failures.

The Pharisees are long gone, but their influence remains. Today, each one of us has our own "inner Pharisee." We each have our own ideas about what is right and wrong, and if someone fails to measure up to our standard, our inner Pharisee will quickly condemn them. This was true of the people to whom James was writing as well. They had learned well the judgmental attitude of the Pharisees and adopted it as their own.

In James' letter, we have observed the people as they struggled in their relationships. Some of them were fighting with each other, jealous of each other, and selfish about their lives and ministries. They thought they were better than other people and routinely judged them. As a

> *The law of Christ requires us to love one another, exercising our freedom in Christ in a way that does not cause a fellow-believer to stumble.*

result, they used harsh words that flowed from a critical spirits. Ultimately, this is one of the painful manifestations of pride (4:6-10).

In today's text we learn that living with a judgmental attitude is contrary to God's will for our lives. James begins by addressing the problem of slander. We've observed him address this problem elsewhere (1:26; 2:4; 3:9, 14, 16; 4:1). James teaches that this kind of speech is a by-product of a judgmental attitude. The process works like this: When we see people do things with which we disapprove, we judge them in our hearts. This is an act of pride, because we have set ourselves in a position of authority over them. Then, we reach a verdict about their actions and character. Finally, we punish them with our words by criticizing, slandering, or gossiping about them.

James argues against this practice by reminding us that God is the only one with the authority to both establish the law and then judge people by it. When we judge people by our own standards, we are taking God's role as our own. In pride, we are living as if we are God, supposing that our thoughts and plans are better than his.

Today, however, the Old Testament ceremonial laws no longer bind us; we now submit to the perfect law of Christ. The law of Christ requires us to love one another, exercising our freedom in Christ in a way that does not cause a fellow-believer to stumble (Jn 13:34; 1 Cor 8:12-13).

Jesus himself had much to say about judging. One of his most famous teachings on the subject is found in Matthew 7:1, "Judge not, that you be not judged." In this verse, he is emphasizing how foolish it is for us to judge others. In reality, we regularly look past our own faults while we are cataloging the faults of others. Jesus calls this the height of hypocrisy—the curse of the inner Pharisee. God alone is capable of being both lawgiver and judge, because he alone is sinless. When we embrace the law of Christ, we allow God to do his work as lawgiver and judge, and we are free to love one another in his name.

That said, the Bible teaches us that judging our neighbor is a sin, but exercising discernment in regards to our neighbor is a virtue. How can both of these statements be true? How can we exercise discernment without judging? The key to answering these questions lies in the meaning and motive of the words themselves. The word judge means to reach conclusions based on the actions of others. When we judge someone else, we are making determinations about whether they are doing right or wrong, often on the basis of our inner Pharisees' personal code of conduct.

Discernment, on the other hand, is perception informed by wisdom. When we exercise discernment, we are making determinations about whether our own choices are right or wrong, and these determinations are based on the truth found in God's word. As you can see, there is a huge difference between these two definitions and motives. Judging is foolish, because it assumes that we are the source of truth for life. Discernment is wise, because it applies God's truth to our lives.

How does this process work you ask? Here are some practical suggestions for cultivating discernment in your life. First, discernment is based upon God's truth, not personal preference. God determines what is right or wrong, and we must allow his word to shape our personal choices. Second, we must be willing to allow God's truth to become truth for us. We will never be able to make the correct decisions for our lives if we do not submit to Scripture. Third, discernment equips us to make correct decisions when confronted with the choices of others. It allows us to make decisions about others, but only on the basis of their ac-

We regularly look past our own faults while we are cataloguing the faults of others.

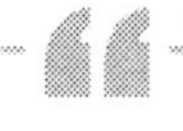

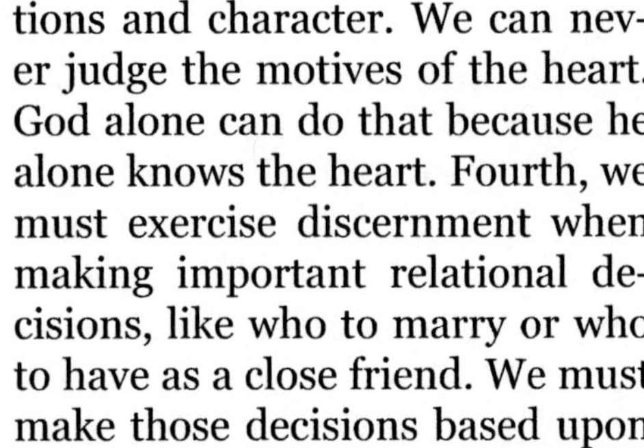

If we're not careful, our pursuit of holiness can turn from an act of worship to an idol of legalism.

tions and character. We can never judge the motives of the heart. God alone can do that because he alone knows the heart. Fourth, we must exercise discernment when making important relational decisions, like who to marry or who to have as a close friend. We must make those decisions based upon the discernment we develop from our knowledge of God's truth found in the Bible. Fifth, and finally, we must remember that it is a very short leap from discernment to judging. If we're not careful, our pursuit of holiness can turn from an act of worship to an idol of legalism. This false step will empower our inner Pharisee to judge the lives of others.

James ends our text for today with these words, "Who are you to judge your neighbor?" Now, we can correctly answer his question. We are totally incapable of judging others, because we have neither the ability nor the expertise—only God can do this. Furthermore, judging others reveals the pride in our own hearts, whereby we maximize the sins of others while minimizing our own sins. Finally, judging sets aside the law of Christ, which requires us to love one another.

Food for Thought

We all struggle with judging others, because we all struggle with pride. We spend a significant amount of time every day judging the people around us. We judge them for what they wear, what they do, what they say, where they go, and for a thousand other things. Sometimes, we judge them because their actions are wrong. Often, however, their actions are not wrong; they're just different. When we judge their actions, we may also judge their motives. We feel confident that we know "why" they do what they do. Finally, we often talk to other people about them, occasionally with disparaging remarks. Why do you think we spend so much time judging others? Is it possible to "love our neighbor as ourselves" when we do this? Why is God so passionate about driving this sin out of our hearts?

Faith in Action

Try to count how may times you judge someone today. It will probably begin the moment you leave your house for your drive to work or school. Make a note every time you do it on a piece of paper or in the note app on your phone. When you note it, pause to think about the strength of your inner Pharisee. Try to identify the sin in your own life that you're ignoring when you point out the sin in someone else's life.

Prayer

In your prayer time today, talk with God about the reality of your own inner Pharisee. Ask God to make you aware today of how often you judge others. Then, ask God to teach you how to submit to the law of liberty so that you can love your neighbors in such a way that you lead them to a personal relationship with Jesus.

James 4:13-17

Come now, you who say, "Today or tomorrow we will go into such and such a town and spend a year there and trade and make a profit"—yet you do not know what tomorrow will bring. What is your life? For you are a mist that appears for a little time and then vanishes. Instead you ought to say, "If the Lord wills, we will live and do this or that." As it is, you boast in your arrogance. All such boasting is evil. So whoever knows the right thing to do and fails to do it, for him it is sin.

"If you aim at nothing, you'll hit it every time." I've heard this famous proverb for years. It resonates with me, because I'm a planner. If you have no plans or goals, you will accomplish nothing, and you will succeed at nothing. The Bible has much to say about the value of planning. One of my favorite texts on this theme is from Proverbs 6:6-11,

> "Go to the ant, O sluggard; consider her ways, and be wise. Without having any chief, officer, or ruler, she prepares her bread in summer and gathers her food in harvest. How long will you lie there, O sluggard? When will you arise from your sleep? A little sleep, a little slumber, a little folding of the hands to rest, and poverty will come upon you like a robber, and want like an armed man."

Here, a wise person and a foolish person are contrasted, and the distinguishing difference is the capacity to plan. Like the ants, wise people make plans, set goals, and experience success. Foolish people, however, drift aimless-

We live like "practical atheists" when we claim to know God but we do not include him in our planning.

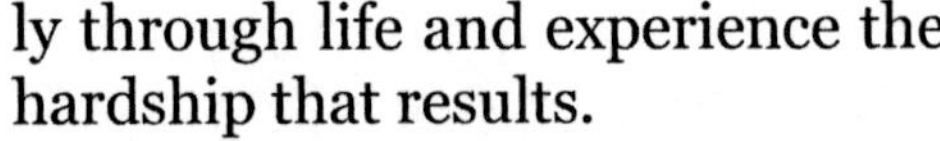

ly through life and experience the hardship that results.

In today's text, James is challenging his people to think rightly about the process of planning the affairs of daily life. When we first read it, it sounds as if James is minimizing the significance of planning. In actuality, James is teaching us about the motive behind our planning. He begins by describing some business owners who are making plans to expand into a new territory. The management team has already done its logistical work, and its time to launch the plan. The goal is simple: make money. At face value, there's nothing wrong with this plan. In fact, it reflects strategic thinking and a good business model.

Yet, for the Christian in business, it's missing the key ingredient—an awareness of God's sovereign purpose. So, James asks and answers this question: "What is your life? You are a mist that appears for a little time and then vanishes." Here, James is teaching two key principles. First, it is arrogant and foolish to leave God out of our plans. None of us has the ability to see the future. We can make projections and contingency plans, but we cannot control the next minute, let alone the next year. When we leave God out of our plans, we're really acting as if we're the ones who are in control of our futures. This is a faulty assumption. Second, it is arrogant and foolish to live without a keen awareness of our own mortality. Life is fragile and brief. We all act and plan like we'll live forever, even though we know this isn't the case. When we leave God out of our planning, we're really acting like we are in control of our fate. This, too, is a faulty assumption.

In reality, we live like "practical atheists" when we claim to know God but we do not include him in our planning. Many Christians include God in their thoughts and plans on Sunday but exclude him from the other days of their week. God's plans for our lives are holistic, however. His plans encompass our lives, marriages, families, careers, and even our hobbies. Consequently, he wants to be involved in every area of our lives, and it is arrogant and foolish to think we can ignore him.

Thankfully, James provides us with practical instruction about how to do this in the following verses. He writes, "Instead you ought to say, "If the Lord wills, we will live and do this or that." With these words, James reminds us of the simple reality that God is sovereign over all things, including our plans. When we say that God is sovereign, we're acknowledging that he is in control of everything in his creation. Here, James teaches his third principle: It is wise to surrender our plans to God's sovereignty. The business plan discussed in verse 13 is a great one, with one exception—it has not been surrendered to God in a spirit of humility. For a Christian, planning has two parts. The first part is technical. The actual design of the plan requires time, effort, study, preparation, and wisdom. The second part is spiritual. This is the point in the process where the plan is surrendered to God and his will. True surrender to God acknowledges that he is sovereign over the days of our lives and the success of our plans.

If we skip this critical part of the planning process, we are allowing pride to control our hearts. James continues, "As it is, you boast in your arrogance. All such boasting is evil. So whoever knows the right thing to do and fails to do it, for him it is sin." James is building on his teaching from earlier in this chapter. Pride tempts us to plan our lives apart from acknowledging God's sovereignty. It tempts us to believe that we are the source of our abilities and successes. Yet, it is arrogant and boastful to live like this, because it is a clear rejection of God's truth, and that is always sin.

This leads us to James' fourth principle: it is wise to acknowledge God as the source of our abilities and provision. Our

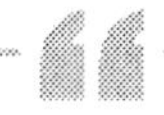

True surrender to God acknowledges that he is sovereign over the days of our lives and the success of our plans.

"If the Lord wills" isn't a mantra—it's a way of life.

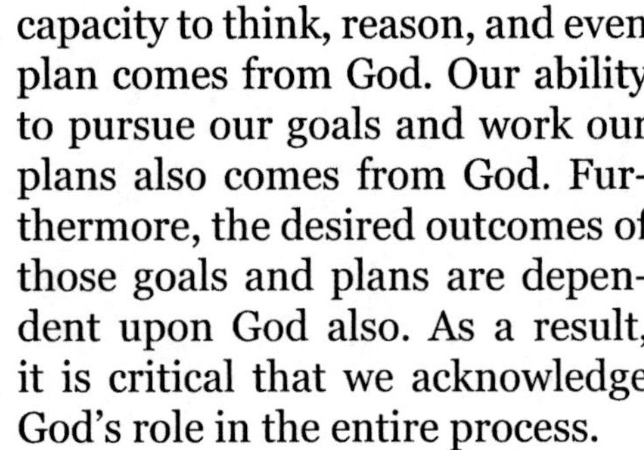

capacity to think, reason, and even plan comes from God. Our ability to pursue our goals and work our plans also comes from God. Furthermore, the desired outcomes of those goals and plans are dependent upon God also. As a result, it is critical that we acknowledge God's role in the entire process.

Ultimately, surrender to God's will isn't a matter of semantics; the phrase "If the Lord wills" isn't a mantra—it's a way of life. It is the Christian's way of both viewing the world and living in it. Living with this worldview requires us to acknowledge God in every area of our lives, to submit to his will, and to make the pursuit of his glory the ultimate goal of life.

Food for Thought

Think about your "to-do" list for today. What do you have planned? Now, look at it again. Have you invited God into the process of planning your day? Of course, God will not write your to-do list for you; planning is your job. But, have you surrendered these plans to God today? Have you acknowledged before God that he is sovereign over your life and your plans? Have you asked for wisdom and strength as you pursue your goals? Have you asked for God's favor on your plans?

Faith in Action

How can you design your plans in the future to reflect a heart that is surrendered to God's sovereignty? Consider designing a to-do list that has two columns. In the left column, create a space to write the tasks of the day. In the right column, create a space to write prayer needs related to those tasks. Leave room at the bottom for a reminder to commit your plans to the Lord (Ps 37:5; Pr 3:5-6).

Prayer

Your prayer time today provides you with a great opportunity to practice the principles from today's text. Talk with God about all of your plans. Ask him for wisdom and strength. Surrender your plans to his sovereign will, and commit your heart to trust him with the outcomes.

James 5:1-6

Come now, you rich, weep and howl for the miseries that are coming upon you. Your riches have rotted and your garments are moth-eaten. Your gold and silver have corroded, and their corrosion will be evidence against you and will eat your flesh like fire. You have laid up treasure in the last days. Behold, the wages of the laborers who mowed your fields, which you kept back by fraud, are crying out against you, and the cries of the harvesters have reached the ears of the Lord of hosts. You have lived on the earth in luxury and in self-indulgence. You have fattened your hearts in a day of slaughter. You have condemned and murdered the righteous person. He does not resist you.

Recently, my wife and I completed a sabbatical trip through Germany. While there, we toured the cities where the Reformer Martin Luther lived and labored. During our trip, we visited Wartburg Castle, where Luther was sequestered by Frederick the Wise following his dramatic testimony at the Diet of Worms. Luther wrote some of his most significant works at Wartburg Castle, including his translation of the New Testament from Greek into German in a mere 11 weeks; a feat which not only gave the Bible to the German people but also provided the first codified grammar of the German language.

Wartburg Castle is a magnificent structure that towers above the surrounding area. It is filled with reminders of a bygone era; an era filled with kings and emperors. The primary meeting hall is graced by hand carved ceilings, beautiful tapestries, and famous paintings. It is opulent even by today's standards. One can only imagine how much wealth it represented in the 16th century. While this magnificent castle remains, the landscape of Germany is littered with the ruins of other castles—crumbling reminders of power and money now lost to memory.

In yesterday's devotion, James challenged us to invite God into the plans and goals of our lives. Interestingly, he used an example from business to teach us this truth. In doing so, he reveals that it isn't a sin to make plans that include the accumulation of financial resources. Today, he will challenge us to think rightly about the way we make and spend that money. James begins by describing the businessperson who lives his life and manages his business without God. He neither submits to God's will nor his ethics. He is willing to do whatever it takes to make money, even if it means taking advantage of the people who work for him. Consequently, he is able to live a life of luxury and self-indulgence.

James sounds a warning to all those who consider making this fatal mistake. He begins by reminding us of the inevitable decay of all material things. I often ride through small towns in South Carolina. When I do, I see the grand houses of days gone by collapsing into ruin, much like the old castles in Germany. Nothing in this world lasts forever. Next, he reminds us that money is often easier to attain than retain. Not only does the cost of living erode our net worth, but so too does the risk of investing. The stock and housing market collapses at the beginning of the 21st century prove that holding on to wealth is often an illusive pursuit. Finally, he reminds us that God will judge the wicked in part on the basis of how they accumulated and spent their money. He writes, "Your gold and silver have corroded, and their corrosion will be evidence against you and will eat your flesh like fire. You have laid up treasure in the last days." They lived in luxury during their lives, while those who served them suffered. One day, their wealth will stand in judgment against them, and they will suffer God's judgment forever.

We shouldn't be filled with pride when we view our possessions, nor should we place our trust in riches—they can be gone in an instant!

History is littered with the names of great kings and business tycoons, men who built empires upon the sacrifices and service of others, accumulating great fortunes in the process. They all have one thing in common—they're dead. The houses they built are curiosities for tourists, if they exist at all. Their money has long since passed into the hands of others, and their personal possessions, if any remain, collect dust in museums. Today, they weep in hell and mourn the choices of their lives; choices for which they will one day give an account to God.

Nowhere does God say that it is a sin to accumulate money as a believer, but he does provide the following guidelines for its use. "As for the rich in this present age, charge them not to be haughty, nor to set their hopes on the uncertainty of riches, but on God, who richly provides us with everything to enjoy. They are to do good, to be rich in good works, to be generous and ready to share, thus storing up treasure for themselves as a good foundation for the future, so that they may take hold of that which is truly life (1 Tim 6:17-19). These verses provide the antidote to the wasted life described in today's text. Here, God uses Paul to provide us with the proper way to think about our money.

First, we must acknowledge that our ability to make money comes from God. As a result, we shouldn't be filled with pride when we view our possessions, nor should we place our trust in riches—they can be gone in an instant!

Second, we must commit ourselves to live according to God's purpose and ethics. In doing so we must submit our money to God for his kingdom work. Of course, this begins with our tithe, but it expands to include numerous other ministry opportunities. Paul describes this as "doing

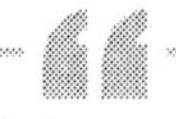

God has provided us with the things we have to enjoy. As a result, we can be generous with all that God has given to us.

good, being rich in good works, and being generous and ready to share." The rich guy described by James will hoard his money for personal pleasure, unconcerned about the needs of those around him. As Christians, however, we embrace a different ethic. We understand that God has provided us with the things we have to enjoy. As a result, we can be generous with all that God has given to us, looking for opportunities to bless those around us who have needs. Further, we can invest in God's larger kingdom work by giving generously to missions and church planting for the spreading of the gospel.

Third, and finally, when we follow God's guidelines for our finances, we are "storing up treasure for ourselves as a good foundation for the future, so that we may take hold of that which is truly life (1 Tim 6:19)." Paul learned this truth from Jesus, who taught, "Do not lay up for yourselves treasures on earth, where moth and rust destroy and where thieves break in and steal, but lay up for yourselves treasure in heaven, where neither moth nor rust destroys and where thieves do not break in and steal. For where your treasure is, there your heart will be also (Mt 6:19-21)." Unlike the man whose treasures torment him in hell, the believer who lays up treasure in heaven will enjoy them for all eternity.

We are all rich when we consider the situation of most of the people in our world. As a result, we must pause to consider if we're honoring God with our money. The following questions will help us keep our financial focus.

1. Whom do we serve—God or money? Jesus said it is impossible to serve both (Mt 6:24). If we make financial decisions without involving God in the process, we are living with false loyalties. We must love and serve God with our money.

2. What do we value—people or things? We've already seen that valuing our possessions is a fatal mistake. Yet, when we fail to use our financial resources to meet the needs we encounter in God's kingdom, we're really saying that we value our money more than the people around us who need the gospel
3. Where does our treasure reside—in heaven or on earth? The most important portfolio we possess is not the one that reveals our net worth here on earth. Rather, it is the one that measures the amount of resources we are investing in God's kingdom, which begins here and continues into eternity.

These questions are convicting, because they challenge the way we think about our money. They come with an amazing promise, however. When we submit our money to God for his purposes, we not only have resources to invest in his kingdom, we have good things to enjoy also. And, we will have treasure waiting for us one day when we arrive in heaven!

> *"When we submit our money to God for his purposes, we not only have resources to invest in his kingdom, we have good things to enjoy also."*

Food for Thought

Today, you've seen two ways that you can live your life. The first way abandons both God and his will. It may produce some measure of earthly, financial success, but it ends in eternal ruin. The second way embraces both God and his will. It, too, may produce some measure of earthly, financial success, but it ends in eternal blessing. Spend some time reflecting on these two ways to live your life. Do you live like the person described in James or in Timothy? How would God describe your current lifestyle? Would he be pleased with how you manage your money or would he be disappointed?

Faith in Action

Today, make a quick review of your personal finances. Can you see the specific places where you are laying up treasure in heaven? Are you faithful in giving 10% of your gross income to God through your church? Are you giving something above your tithe to other kingdom ventures, like supporting a church planter or missionary? How about your generosity? Are you regularly helping others who may have financial needs or supporting your fellow believers who are serving in short-term missions projects? If so, you are honoring God through your finances. If not, today is the day to submit your finances to God, so that you can begin to invest in his kingdom and lay up treasure in heaven.

Prayer

As you pray today, talk with God about the situation surrounding your finances. Talk with him about your needs as you ask for his favor. Commit yourself anew to be a faithful steward of your financial resources. Ask God to make you aware of the people around you to whom you can show generosity, and ask him to provide you with additional resources that you can use for his glory.

James 5:7-8

Be patient, therefore, brothers until the coming of the Lord. See how the farmer waits for the precious fruit of the earth, being patient about it, until it receives the early and the late rains. You also, be patient. Establish your hearts, for the coming of the Lord is at hand.

Is there anything more difficult to cultivate in our lives than patience? Sadly, I can think of a thousand different ways I have been impatient—and that was just yesterday! All kidding aside, it is a daily struggle to live with patience. We're impatient when the slow driver refuses to yield the fast lane, when our business meeting is rescheduled, or when our flight is delayed. We're impatient when our spouses don't meet our expectations, when our children are late getting ready for school, or when our friends are late for dinner. Honestly, we have the capacity to be impatient about anything.

We all struggle with patience because we're all selfish. We often live as if the world revolves around us. As a result, we want everyone and everything to yield to our plans and timeline. When they fail to do so, we become impatient. Impatience is just a symptom of a larger problem, however; it is one of the manifestations of anger. Anger can manifest itself in many ways: it can produce a passive aggressive silence or a glass-breaking rage. Often, however, it produces the frustration and rising blood pressure that is connected with impatience.

The real question that begs to be answered is this: where does anger come from? Anger, which is a common

human problem, results from our pride. Do you remember our study of James 1:19-21? There, we learned that pride leads us to believe that we are in control of the circumstances of our lives. The word we use to describe this is "autonomy;" it means freedom from the control of others. At its core, it means that we want what we want, how we want it, and when we want it. Our autonomy is threatened when something interferes with our desires. This causes us to become angry, and when this happens, it often manifests itself through impatience.

We usually don't associate impatience with anger, but they are connected like a light bulb and electricity—one can't function without the other. Think back to the last time you felt impatient because someone was making you late. In reality, you were angry with them for disrupting your schedule. Can you remember the questions swirling around in your mind? "Why is he late again? How hard is it to get ready on time? Doesn't he own a clock?" Now, think about all of the other things that make us impatient. They all flow out of anger, and anger always results when our sense of personal autonomy is threatened. Yet, selfish pride is our real enemy.

Our text for today begins the final section of James' book. In this final section, he provides us with some final words of admonition and encouragement in light of all that he has already taught. As a result, it's not unusual that he begins with patience. If you think back over the previous days of this study, James dealt with many things that can make us impatient: adversity, financial problems, inconsiderate people, faithless people, profane people, selfish people, and proud people (can you feel the irony of this one?). When we are impatient with people or circumstances like these in our own lives, the root is always anger.

So, how do we overcome our inherent battle with anger and the resulting impatience that plagues our days? James gives a simple answer: "Be patient, therefore, brothers until the coming of the Lord." Really? That's the answer? Yes, really. The word that is used here for patience means to persevere in the face of adversity. This is the opposite of hasty anger, which is another way to describe impatience. James is teaching us that patience should define our lives until we return to Christ or he returns for us. In other words, there is not time in our lives when impatience should define us. I have to confess something here. When I read this text I feel somewhat like a failure. There is no doubt that God sends us lots of trials and people to teach us patience. Yet, while I've had lots of practice, I feel that I continue to struggle to grow in this area of my life. Maybe you can identify with that feeling.

Next, James provides us with an analogy from agriculture to help us understand how patience really works. He writes, "See how the farmer waits for the precious fruit of the earth, being patient about it, until it receives the early and the late rains." I never really understood the significance of these words until I moved to a farm several years ago. One fall, I planted dozens of blueberry bushes. I spent days on my hands and knees planting them. Then, I waited for them to grow and bear fruit.

Until then, I had never focused much attention on the weather. In fact, I was often disappointed when it rained because it altered my plans. Now, I'm grateful for every drop of rain that falls on the farm. One year passed, and then another. In year three my plants finally began to produce berries. Now, my blueberry field provides an annual yield, but the quality of fruit is always affected by the quantity of rain we receive. Through this process, I've finally learned what James was teaching—farming takes patience and so does life.

Patience means to persevere in the face of adversity.

James 5:7-8

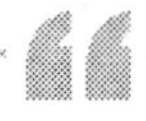

God hides divine appointments in the most surprising places.

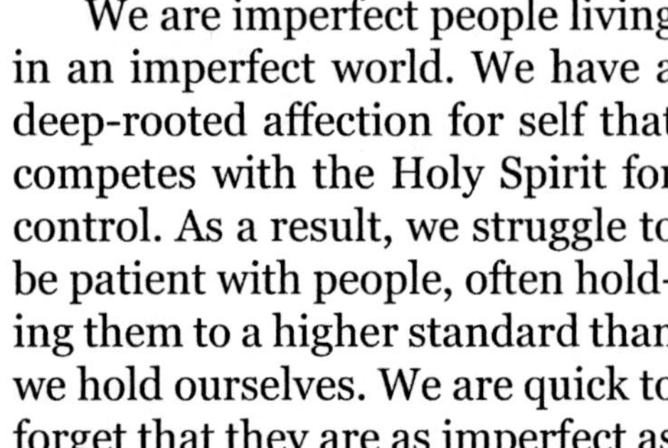

We are imperfect people living in an imperfect world. We have a deep-rooted affection for self that competes with the Holy Spirit for control. As a result, we struggle to be patient with people, often holding them to a higher standard than we hold ourselves. We are quick to forget that they are as imperfect as we. How, then, are we to accomplish this, for it seems as if God has given us an impossible task—to model his patience in this broken world.

James reveals that this is a spiritual task, and we can only accomplish it in the power of God's Holy Spirit. He writes, "Establish your hearts, for the coming of the Lord is at hand." This language refers to the journey of discipleship—it is the daily pursuit of God's glory revealed through a life of obedience. The motivation for establishing our hearts daily is the reality of the imminent return of Christ.

As we walk with Christ daily through the power of the Holy Spirit, we will find that we are capable of exercising patience in even the most difficult of circumstances. It will still be a challenge, however. Here are some practical things to remember today when you are tempted to be impatient. First, begin each day by acknowledging God's sovereignty over your plans (4:15). This prayer prepares you to accept God's disruption of your plans with grace. Second, view every inconvenience as a divine opportunity to model the gospel by showing grace to others (Phil 2:13). Third, choose to respond to situations that make you angry and impatient in a way that would please God. Often, God hides divine appointments in the most surprising places. So, when you're tempted to be impatient today, remember—God may have an amazing spiritual adventure planned just for you!

Food for Thought

Spend some time thinking about the things that make you the most impatient. How would you categorize them? Are they family issues? Career issues? Technology issues? Are there certain people who test your patience the most? Are there certain times of the day when patience is harder to demonstrate? Now, consider the anger issues that may be at the root of some of these situations. Why do they make you angry? Who can you talk to about these areas to receive some wise counsel? How can you submit these areas of your heart to the lordship of Jesus?

Faith in Action

Chances are you will be tempted to be impatient before you get an hour into your day. This will provide you with a great opportunity to apply what you've learned from God's word today. Remember the three-step process: a) commit your plans to the Lord; b) remember that every interruption to your personal schedule is a potential divine appointment; c) respond to the things that could make you impatient with a grace that pleases God and blesses others.

Prayer

It's been said that you shouldn't pray for patience, because if you do, the Lord will certainly provide you with more opportunities to practice. Truth is, however, that we do need God's help to grow in this area of our lives. So, spend some time praying about your responses to adversity in your life today.

James 5:9-11

Do not grumble against one another, brothers, so that you may not be judged; behold, the Judge is standing at the door. As an example of suffering and patience, brothers, take the prophets who spoke in the name of the Lord. Behold, we consider those blessed who remained steadfast. You have heard of the steadfastness of Job, and you have seen the purpose of the Lord, how the Lord is compassionate and merciful.

Most of the regrettable things I've said were spoken when anger made me impatient, and I took out my frustration on the people around me—often the most important people in my life. Isn't that the way it works, though? Anger grips our hearts because our autonomy is threatened, and we become impatient. Then, hurtful or hateful words pour out of our mouths, and any chance to be a distributor of God's grace in that moment is lost forever.

Yesterday, James introduced the issue of patience and its importance in our lives. It is important, initially, because it is a character trait of God (Rom 9:22-24). These verses in Romans teach us that God is patient with sinners, because he loves them and wants to save them. It also reveals another reason that patience is important—it is an evidence of love. In 1 Corinthians 13:5-8 Paul writes a beautiful description of the attributes of godly love. Guess what's

There is nothing more beautiful than a patient, trusting, and surrendered saint.

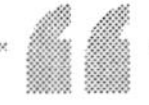

There are few things more unattractive than an angry, impatient, and complaining Christians.

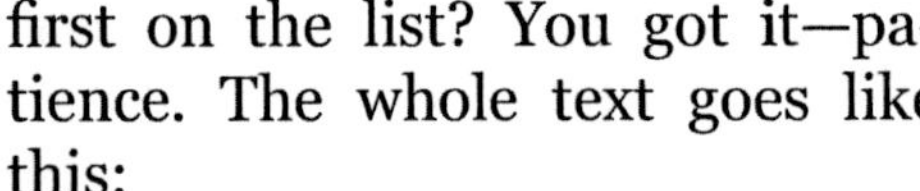

first on the list? You got it—patience. The whole text goes like this:

"Love is patient and kind; love does not envy or boast; it is not arrogant or rude. It does not insist on its own way; it is not irritable or resentful; it does not rejoice at wrongdoing, but rejoices with the truth. Love bears all things, believes all things, hopes all things, endures all things. Love never ends." This text reveals that when God's love is working in us to produce patience, we inevitably treat people with kindness (Eph 4:32). But, should anger and impatience define us, we are capable of the worst kind of speech and behavior (James 3:1-12).

In today's text, James concludes his teaching on the danger of impatience to our relationships and witness. Notice his primary admonition, "Do not grumble." The word grumble here means to be squeezed or to groan or sigh in a difficult situation. It was a word that was used to describe complaining about the people or situations we encounter daily. Think about some of the ways that life can "squeeze" us. We can be squeezed by time. We have a plan for our day, and then someone or something throws a wrench into the works, and suddenly our whole schedule is undone. Or, we find ourselves being squeezed by the priorities of life. Something needs to be done that we don't want to do (like cleaning the garage or the house) and it ends up taking the place of something that we really do want to do (like hunting or shopping). Perhaps we are actually planning to do something that we'd like to do, but nothing goes according to plan, and the day collapses around us in ruin (like when it rains all day at the amusement park—sound familiar?). All of these types of circumstances may threaten our autonomy. If we're not walking in the Spirit, we may become angry and impatient, and grumbling will not be far behind.

Next, James identifies the focus of our grumbling—"against one another." This is relational language. Generally, my impatience is not directed against inanimate objects, although I've been known to get pretty aggravated with my computer! Most often, my impatience is directed at the person or people I perceive to be responsible for "squeezing my life" by affecting my plans in some way. If you are married and have children, this is the place where you will feel squeezed most often, simply because you are with them more than anyone else. A child can lay waste to a carefully laid plan faster than anyone, and 99% of the time, they do it completely by accident. Nevertheless, it can still give rise to anger and impatience. We can experience these same types of things in our other relationships as well. Sadly, it can even occur in our churches, as was the case for James. If we're not careful, we may become self-absorbed in our churches just like we do in the other areas of our lives. We may become impatient about things that don't resonate with our personal preferences, and soon we're grumbling and complaining to those we feel are responsible for the situation. This is extremely detrimental to the effectiveness of the church, and it can often lead to God's discipline.

There are few things more unattractive than angry, impatient, and complaining Christians. At best they are a hindrance to the church; at worst they are tares among the wheat in need of authentic conversion. On the other hand, there is nothing more beautiful than a patient, trusting, and surrendered saint. This is the goal to which God calls each of us. Keep this in mind: If Christians are not striving to patiently love one another in authentic community, the discipline of God is close as hand.

> *God's mercy and compassion is always at work breathing life into dead things, even through the most unlikely of circumstances.*

James provides us with two great examples of people who modeled patience in the presence of suffering—the Old Testament

> *Resting in God's sovereignty prepares us to model grace to those around us, so that they may be drawn to Jesus Christ through the gospel.*

prophets and Job. Most of us cannot fully understand all that James is referring to here. Honestly, we think we're suffering if we get stopped by all of the traffic lights on the way to work, or if our neighbor doesn't keep his yard properly groomed. James is talking about people whose plans and goals were altered by real problems--like persecution or tragedy. Despite this, both Job and the prophets trusted in God's sovereign will for their lives, and both were faithful to God's word.

Both encountered real suffering and responded with patience and endurance. We look back with awe when we consider all that they accomplished for God in such difficult situations. How were they able to accomplish that which we find so difficult? James gives us the answer—they lived with a profound faith in God's compassion and mercy. They understood that God had a plan for their lives, trusted God to guide their steps, (even if it meant interrupting their plans), and believed that God's mercy and compassion is always at work breathing life into dead things, even through the most unlikely of circumstances (Phil 1:12-18).

Before we conclude our study today, there is one small phrase that demands our attention. Tucked away in the middle of these verses is a beautiful statement. James writes, "We consider those blessed who remained steadfast." Here, he links the end of his book to the very first verses of his book. Do you remember day two of our study? There, we read these words, "Count it all joy, my brothers, when you meet trials of various kinds, for you know that the testing of your faith produces steadfastness (James 1:2-3)." James uses the exact same word in chapter one that we find in our text today. The word "steadfast" means endurance. Finally, we see how the whole process comes together. Patience, which is motivated by godly love and made possible by the power of the Holy Spirit, equips us to live with endurance. Endurance leads to the development of spiritual maturity. Spiritual maturity equips us to rest in God's sovereignty, even when we fail to understand all that God is doing in our lives. And, resting in God's sovereignty prepares us to model grace to those around us, so that they may be drawn to Jesus Christ through the gospel.

Food for Thought

Life has a way of squeezing us. Often, this is simply the result of trying to do too many things. No sets out to overwhelm themselves; it happens subtly over time. Still, we will struggle with patience when we get to the place where we're having trouble managing all of life's demands. What about you? Are you feeling squeezed in some area of your life today? What is causing it? How does it make you feel? How are you responding to it—with grace and patience or with grumbling and impatience?

Faith in Action

It's easier to combat a known enemy than an unknown one. Sometimes, just identifying an area of our lives where we're struggling with patience is 50% of overcoming it. Name that problem today and think about how you can manage that area of your life with patience. There still may be something else you need to do, however. It could be that you have too much going on in your life. It could be that you need to back off of some things and give your life some margin (consider reading Richard Swenson's book, Margin, after you finish this study in James).

Prayer

If you're struggling to be patient in a difficult circumstance, or just struggling with patience in general, talk with God about it today. Submit yourself to the Holy Spirit, and commit the situation to God's care. Ask for the wisdom to respond rightly when you are tempted to become impatient.

James 5:12

But above all, my brothers, do not swear, either by heaven or by earth or by any other oath, but let your yes be yes and your no be no, so that you may not fall under condemnation.

It's hard to keep a secret. Do you remember trying to keep a secret when you were young? If you're like me, you may have struggled with that. I can remember one of my friends telling me that he liked a girl in our class, but he was too embarrassed to let anyone know—including her! He asked me not to tell anyone, and I agreed. Perhaps he was concerned about my ability to do this, however, because he said, "Swear to me on the Bible that you won't tell anyone." That, of course, put it in a different perspective and helped me understand that he was totally serious about this information remaining secret.

People have been making oaths like this for millennia. Oaths, by definition, are promises to fulfill a pledge, whether it's to keep a secret or to accomplish a task. The value of the oath is often determined by the value of the object upon which the oath is sworn. So, people swear by themselves, a stack of Bibles, their mother's grave, the souls of their children, and by God himself. As you can see, these oaths demonstrate increasing value, with God being the highest authority by which one may swear.

Oaths are promises to fulfill a pledge, whether it's to keep a secret or to accomplish a task.

The Bible has much to teach us about God's view of swearing oaths. Consider these verses:

- Ex 20:7 – "You shall not take the name of the LORD your God in vain, for the LORD will not hold him guiltless who takes his name in vain."
- Lev 19:12 – "You shall not swear by my name falsely, and so profane the name of your God: I am the LORD."
- Num 30:2 – "If a man vows a vow to the LORD, or swears an oath to bind himself by a pledge, he shall not break his word. He shall do according to all that proceeds out of his mouth."
- Eccl 5:4-6 – "When you vow a vow to God, do not delay paying it, for he has no pleasure in fools. Pay what you vow. It is better that you should not vow than that you should vow and not pay. Let not your mouth lead you into sin, and do not say before the messenger that it was a mistake. Why should God be angry at your voice and destroy the work of your hands?"

As you can see, the Old Testament law forbade irreverent oaths, light use of the Lord's name, and broken vows, because once God's name was invoked, the vow to which it was attached became a debt that must be paid.

In Jesus' day, the Pharisees had devised an ingenious system of loopholes to avoid keeping one's vows. For instance, if you swore *by* Jerusalem you were not bound to your oath, but if you swore *to* Jerusalem you were bound to your oath. This allowed people to look spiritual while they embraced dishonesty. Notice what Jesus said about this practice in Mt 23:18-19, "And you who say, 'If anyone swears by the altar, it is nothing, but if anyone swears by the gift that is on the altar, he is bound by his oath.' You blind men! For which is greater, the gift or the altar that makes the gift sacred? So whoever swears by

> *Oaths are necessary only in an environment where people don't keep their word.*

the altar swears by it and by everything on it." Jesus isn't supporting the use of oaths; rather, he is emphasizing the importance of truth.

Oaths are unnecessary for those who speak the truth

If you think about it, oaths are necessary only in an environment where people don't keep their word. We only resort to oaths when we've given someone a reason to doubt the truthfulness of our words. Have you ever disappointed someone because you've failed to keep a commitment? Think about what you said to them the next time you gave them your word. It may have sounded like this: "I promise I won't be late this time;" "I give you my word that I'll be there;" "I swear that we'll play catch tonight when I get home." These oaths all give evidence of past failures with truth telling.

In our text today, James is challenging us to speak the truth, simply and precisely. Consider what the Scripture teaches us about truth telling:

- Ex 20:16 – "You shall not bear false witness against your neighbor."
- Ps 15:1-2 – "O LORD, who shall sojourn in your tent? Who shall dwell on your holy hill? He who walks blamelessly and does what is right and speaks truth in his heart."
- Pr 6:16-19 – "There are six things the LORD hates, seven that are an abomination to him: ...a lying tongue ... a false witness who breathes out lies."
- John 14:6 – "I am the way, and the truth, and the life. No one comes to the Father except through me."
- Eph 4:14 – "Speaking the truth in love, we are to grow up in every way into him who is the head, into Christ."

These verses reveal that God values truth in every area of our lives.

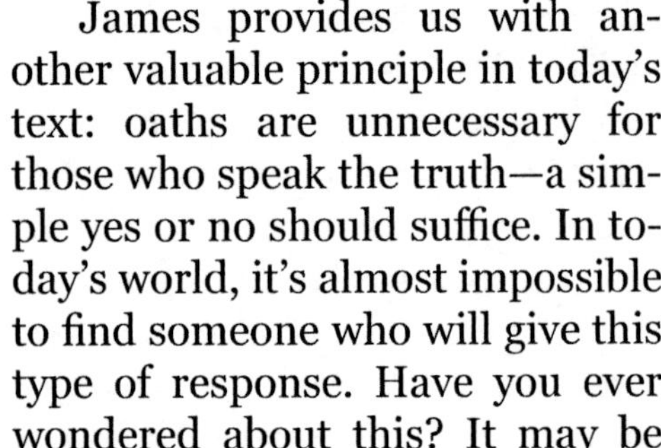

James provides us with another valuable principle in today's text: oaths are unnecessary for those who speak the truth—a simple yes or no should suffice. In today's world, it's almost impossible to find someone who will give this type of response. Have you ever wondered about this? It may be that we're uncomfortable giving a simple yes or no answer when we are asked to do something because it locks us in to a decision. After all, if we say yes, and something else comes along that we would rather do, we are bound by our word. Yet, if we say no, because we really want to do something else, we may be perceived as being unconcerned about a person or situation. This traps us in a dilemma.

Today, of course, we don't swear by the temple, but we have still developed a system that gives us a potential out when we want to hedge on making a commitment. We say, "I may be able attend, let me check my schedule." Or we may say, "I'll have to think about it." Similarly, we may say, "I'll do my best to be there." Sometimes we respond with a spiritual answer, "I'll need to pray about it." There are a hundred variations of this, but all of them are designed to do the same thing—give the appearance that we're going to do something when we know the odds are against it.

Of course, some will say, "What's the harm in this? I don't want to hurt anyone's feelings, and I sure don't want her to think less of me! And, I could actually decide to go." But we recognize this for what it is—a weak excuse. Like the Pharisees, we have become experts of the pseudo-commitment. What really suffers, however, is our integrity. Over time, people begin to assume that we cannot be trusted to do what we say. When that happens, we must resort to oaths in order to convince them that we'll actually honor our commitments. In today's text, God is teaching us that we must be people who both speak and live the truth. If we do otherwise, we are inviting God's discipline into our lives.

How do we accomplish this when we've become so proficient at speaking half-truths? Here are four simple principles: First, we must commit daily to embrace truth in our hearts. Second, we must maintain integrity in our speech so that we need not resort to oaths for people to believe us. Third, we must answer honestly when people ask us for some type of commitment. Remember, it is more important to please God than man. We must let our yes be yes and our no be no. Fourth, we must keep our word even when it hurts. Our word is one of our greatest assets—we must guard it carefully.

Food for Thought

It is hard to find people that you can trust to keep their word. Sadly, this is true even among those who claim to be Christians. How would those who know you describe you? Would they state without reservation that you have integrity when it comes to keeping your word? Or, would they have you on the list of people that they don't trust? Every day, you are building one of those legacies. How can you build a legacy of truth today in this area of your life?

Faith in Action

You will be asked to do things today, and you will need to give some type of response. If possible, give a simple yes or no answer. If, legitimately, you need to check your schedule first, write down the information so that you do not forget to check. Then, once you have looked at your schedule, call the person back and give a definite yes or no answer. Resist every temptation to give an answer that looks like a yes when you really mean no.

Prayer

Only God and you really know the depth of your commitment to truth. Be honest with God today—he really does know the truth anyway. Perhaps you need to confess that your commitment to truth has been weak in this area. Ask for God's forgiveness and help. Further, spend some time talking with God about the challenge of embracing truth in a world where it is devalued. Commit to walk in truth today.

James 5:13-16a

Is there anyone among you suffering? Let him pray. Is anyone cheerful? Let him sing praise. Is anyone among you sick? Let him call for the elders of the church, and let them pray over him, anointing him with oil in the name of the Lord. And the prayer of faith will save the one who is sick, and the Lord will raise him up. And if he has committed sins, he will be forgiven. Therefore, confess your sins to one another and pray for one another, that you may be healed.

Prayer is an amazing gift from God. Think about it—God has given us the privilege of talking with him any time we want! Consider the following verses on prayer:

- Lk 11:2-4 – "And he said to them, "When you pray, say: 'Father, hallowed by your name. Your kingdom come. Give us each day our daily bread, and forgive us our sins, for we ourselves forgive everyone who is indebted to us. And lead us not into temptation.'"
- Rom 8:26 – "Likewise the Spirit helps us in our weakness. For we do not know what to pray for as we ought, but the Spirit himself intercedes for us with groanings too deep for words."
- Phil 4:6 – "Do not be anxious about anything, but in everything by prayer and supplication with thanksgiving let your requests be made known to God. And the peace of God, which surpasses all understanding, will guard your hearts and your minds in Christ Jesus."

- Heb 4:16 – "Let us then with confidence draw near to the throne of grace, that we may receive mercy and find grace to help in time of need."
- 1 Pet 3:12 – "The eyes of the Lord are on the righteous, and his ears are open to their prayer."

These verses reveal that God wants us to talk with him about the circumstances we're facing in our lives, and that he promises to hear us and help us as we pray. Consequently, prayer must be a part of our daily spiritual journey.

In today's text, James teaches us that God intends to use prayer as a gift of grace, in both the good times and the difficult times of our lives. He begins with these simple admonitions: "Is there anyone among you suffering? Let him pray. Is anyone cheerful? Let him sing praise." In these two statements, James covers any situation we may face. Life is a constant journey between these two extremes—suffering and joy.

Our response to both is the same, however. We must pray when we are experiencing the testing of our faith that builds steadfastness (James 1:2-3). These are the moments when we must cast all of our anxieties on Christ, because he cares for us (1 Pet 5:7). And, we must pray when we are experiencing the blessings of faithful labor (Gal 6:9). These are the moments when we must cast all of our praise on him, because he is the one who gives us all things to enjoy (1 Tim 6:17). In other words, we must always pray (1 Thes 5:17).

As James continues, he addresses the need to pray when we are sick. These verses deserve careful attention, because they are often taught incorrectly. James makes the following statement, "Is anyone among you sick? Let him call for the elders of the church, and let them pray over him, anointing him with oil in the name of the Lord. And the prayer of faith will save the one who is sick, and the Lord will raise him up."

> *"Do not be anxious about anything, but in everything by prayer and supplication with thanksgiving let your requests be made known to God."*

There are two important Greek words here that are both translated "sick" in English, but only the first occurrence carries the possible meaning of physical illness. It is the word translated "sick" in verse 14, and it means "to be weak." Sometimes in the Gospels it is used to describe people with physical problems, but generally in the epistles it is used to refer to people who have a weak faith or a weak conscience (Acts 20:35; Rom 6:19; 14:1; 1 Cor 8:9-12). The second word translated "sick" is found in verse 15, and it means "to be weary." This word suggests the weariness of life that accompanies seasons of trial or suffering (James 1:2-3; Heb 12:3).

Prayer must be a part of our daily spiritual journey.

By using these two distinct words, James is revealing that we can pray about any kind of difficulty we may encounter in life. He would include the following challenges of life. First, we must pray when we are confronted by the struggles of physical illness. This isn't the primary meaning of these verses, but we can certainly pray about our seasons of physical suffering. Second, we must pray when we find ourselves battling with temptation. During these times we may be tempted to turn away from God to idols (1 Cor 10:13). Third, we must pray in the face of moral weakness. Prayer is the remedy for overcoming our pet sins, destructive habits, or addictive behaviors. God alone strengthens us to overcome these thorns of the flesh (Rom 7:15-8:11). Fourth, we must pray in seasons of spiritual weakness. Sadly, our weakness may even lead us to wander from the faith in pursuit of sin's pleasures. Prayer is the cure for this loss of focus (Heb 10:19-31). Fifth, and finally, we must pray when we are confronted by persecution. Christians still suffer everyday because of their faith in Jesus. Whether we face ridicule or physical suffering, we must pray for the strength to stand firm (Heb 10:32-39). Each of these situations may cause us to become weak

God responds to these prayers of faith in order to encourage the saints and help them in their suffering.

or feel weary. What should we do when we feel discouraged about one of these areas in our lives? Should we try to tough it out on our own?

No. James tells us to seek the counsel of our Elders (i.e., Pastors) in the church when we're discouraged. Elders have two tasks for dealing with these issues. First, they provide comfort for us through their prayers. When James was an Elder in the church in Jerusalem, oil was used for a variety of purposes. At times, it was applied as a salve designed to promote the healing of skin conditions or wounds. This may be what he is describing in these verses. But oil was also used to maintain one's personal appearance. It was used to provide refreshment and comfort, often being combed into the hair and applied to the face and neck. In this context, the Elders would use oil to demonstrate the grace of God, even as they prayed by faith that God would meet the specific needs in an individual's life. James says that God responds to these prayers of faith in order to encourage the saints and help them in their suffering.

Second, the Elders would provide instruction through their words. James writes, "And if he has committed sins, he will be forgiven. Therefore, confess your sins to one another and pray for one another, that you may be healed." As we noticed above, some seasons of suffering are a result of our own poor choices when we are tempted (James 1:13-15; Heb 12:5-13). When that is the case, it is the role of the Elders to admonish a weak believer so that he will confess his sins and turn to God through repentance. When he does, the Elders will pray with him, and God will give grace and a renewed spirit.

As we conclude today's study, we can derive several valuable principles from this text. First, we must pray. Prayer is a vital part of our spiritual journey, in both good and challenging times. Second, we must pray by faith.

Faith believes in God's promise to provide comfort for us when we are weak or weary. Third, we must practice confession. Sin is often at the root of lifestyle choices that dishonor God and lead to discouragement or depression. Fourth, we must pray for one another. This requires transparency and honesty, but it is necessary so that we can encourage one another in our faith. Fifth, we must seek the counsel and encouragement of our Elders when we are struggling. God intends to use them as a source of blessing, encouragement, and healing in our lives.

Prayer is a vital part of our spiritual journey, in both good and challenging times.

Food for Thought

How would you describe your life today? Are you in a season of joy and celebration? If so, think about your prayers. Do they reflect a spirit of gratitude to God for his kind favor? Or, perhaps, you are in a season of suffering. Do you feel weak or weary in some area of your life? Are you struggling with a temptation or failure that is affecting your spiritual journey? Have you been praying about it? What have you learned today that could help you experience God's grace in your suffering? The Bible makes it clear that prayer is vital to our success as believers. Why, then, is prayer so difficult to practice on a regular basis? Think about your average day. What things often stand in the way of a consistent prayer time for you? Over the past 30 days, you've been asked to spend time in prayer every day. Has this focused emphasis strengthened your prayer life? How?

Faith in Action

Today, I want you to talk about the condition of your spiritual journey with a Christian friend. If you're in a season of joy, share the blessings that God has given you and rejoice in them with your friend. If you're in a season of suffering, share the challenges you're facing and ask your friend to pray for you. If necessary, consider making an appointment to visit with your Elders so that they can provide you with spiritual encouragement.

Prayer

As you pray today, remember that your conversation with God is a special time. You have his undivided attention, so talk with him about all of the needs in your life. Express your gratitude for his good gifts, and confess your sins in humility before him. Guard this time and find joy in God's presence today.

James 5:17-18

The prayer of a righteous person has great power as it is working. Elijah was a man with a nature like ours, and he prayed fervently that it might not rain, and for three years and six months it did not rain on the earth. Then he prayed again, and heaven gave rain, and the earth bore its fruit.

Elijah burst on to the scene in the Old Testament like a thunderbolt. Out of nowhere, this prophet from Tishbe traveled to Samaria, the capital of the northern kingdom of Israel, and proclaimed God's judgment against King Ahab. Ahab was one of the wickedest kings in Israel's history. He married a pagan woman named Jezebel and worshipped her false gods, Baal and Asherah. He built temples in their honor, where the people of Israel participated in the horrific practice of child sacrifice (1 Kg 16:29-33). Elijah said to Ahab, "As the LORD, the God of Israel, lives, before whom I stand, there shall be neither dew nor rain these years, except by my word (1 Kg 17:1)." Then, as quickly as he appeared in Samaria, he was gone into the desert near the Jordan River.

Our faith is not in our own ability to change God's mind or his sovereign purposes. Instead, our faith is in God's ability to accomplish what he has willed.

What followed next was amazing. God used Elijah to accomplish mighty works in Israel and to call the people back from idolatry to himself (1 Kg 17:3-18:40). During that time, the land

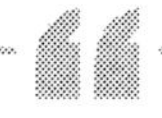

Elijah wasn't perfect, but he was righteous. And so are you if you have a personal relationship with Jesus.

began to suffer the effects of the drought. The streams began to dry up, and water was scarce. Following God's victory over the prophets of the false gods Baal and Asherah, Elijah knew in his spirit that the time had come for the drought to end. The spiritual battle had been won and revival had begun—the land needed rain. So Elijah climbed to the top of Mt. Carmel, bowed before God, and began to pray. After each prayer, he sent his servant to check the sky—nothing. Six times he prayed, and six times he received the same response, "There is nothing." So, he prayed for the seventh time. This time his servant returned with excitement. He said, "Behold, a little cloud like a man's hand is rising from the sea." Elijah leapt to his feet and began to run towards town. God had answered his prayer, and rain was on its way (1 Kg 18:41-46).

In today's text, James concludes his teaching about the importance of prayer by providing Elijah as an example for us. If you're like me, you may feel intimidated when a New Testament writer tells you to imitate the faith of an Old Testament saint. After all, Elijah is one of the greatest prophets in history. How are we supposed to measure up to that? Clearly God isn't going to use us to call down fire from heaven like Elijah did, nor is he going to instruct us to proclaim a drought. So, what can James possibly be trying to teach us here by using Elijah?

To answer this question, we must reflect briefly on our text from yesterday. There, James said, "The prayer of faith will save the one who is sick, and the Lord will raise him up (5:15)." Some have mistakenly interpreted this verse to mean that God will heal anyone's physical illness, as long as the person praying has enough faith. Scripture and experience reveal that this is incorrect. People often die from illnesses; the faith of the person praying cannot change the sovereign will of God. Remember, James was speaking primarily about the way that God responds to our prayers to bring healing to those who are weakened and wearied by the challenges of life. This brings us to our first principle about prayer: Faith is an essential ingredient of our prayers. Our faith is not in our own ability to change God's mind or his sovereign purposes. Instead, our faith is in God's ability to accomplish what he has willed, whether it is to heal the discouraged heart of a friend or to end a drought that has lasted for three-and-a-half years.

As we read today's text, we discover our second principle about prayer: righteousness is an essential ingredient of our prayers. While Elijah may intimidate us, James reveals an important truth—Elijah wasn't a superhero. He was happy and sad, sick and well, encouraged and discouraged, rested and weary, strong and weak—just like us. In fact, after God used him to defeat the pagan prophets of the false gods Baal and Asherah, fear drove him into hiding, and he despaired of life itself. Elijah doesn't sound like much of a spiritual giant, does he?

Yet, Elijah had placed his faith in God and had a personal relationship with him. He pursued God daily, sometimes winning victories and other times suffering defeats. But, he never gave up. He gave glory to God for his successes and asked God's forgiveness for his failures. Elijah wasn't perfect, but he was righteous. And so are you if you have a personal relationship with Jesus. When you placed your faith in Jesus for the forgiveness of your sins, God declared you to be righteous by giving you the righteousness of Jesus. Now, like Elijah, you are a righteous person.

This is important because God only hears the prayers of the righteous. This is why cultivating a lifestyle of personal devotion is so important. We must spend time in the Bible and in prayer so that we stay in right fellowship with God. We must confess our sins daily so

We must spend time in the Bible and in prayer so that we stay in right fellowship with God.

> *The power to overcome adversity by faith is found through the energizing work of the Holy Spirit in our lives.*

that our hearts remain clean before him (Ps 66:18). In doing so, we can live in a way that pleases God and brings him glory. And, we can pray with power.

James writes, "The prayer of a righteous person has great power as it is working." The word translated "power" in this verse is the root word for "energy." It means to work or be active. Literally, it means that energized prayer produces energized results. When we pray by faith as righteous people, God does amazing things both in our lives and the lives of others. Does this mean we'll suddenly have prophetic powers like Elijah? No. Will we suddenly have the gift of healing like the apostles (Acts 3:1-7)? Uh-uh. But, we will have everything that we need to accomplish every task that God has for us through the power of the Holy Spirit (2 Pet 1:3).

Let's observe some final principles about prayer from James 5:13-18. First, all of us experience trials and adversity in our lives. This adversity may take different forms, but it is always designed by God to make us "perfect and complete" in faith (1:4). Our response to this adversity determines the success or failure of our spiritual journey from day to day. Second, when we find that our trials are making us weak or weary, we must pursue God's grace, forgiveness, and strength through prayer. Often, we may need to spend time praying with others, including our church Elders, but this will require us to be honest and transparent about our spiritual needs. Third, the power to overcome adversity by faith is found through the energizing work of the Holy Spirit in our lives. When we submit to him, our lives and our prayers are infused by God's power so that we can fulfill his purposes in our lives.

Food for Thought

The Bible makes it clear that prayer is vital to our success as believers. How does today's text help your understanding of what it means to be a righteous person who prays by faith? You've been challenged to pray every day this month as you've been studying the book of James. In what ways has this daily process challenged you to become more consistent in prayer? How have you seen God at work through your prayers?

Faith in Action

Consider adding a section at the bottom of your "to-do" list form where you can record God's work through your prayers on a daily basis. This section will give you a place to record the ways that you see God work in response to your prayers. It will become the story of your spiritual journey, with its successes and failures. More importantly, it will help build your faith, because it will help you remember all that God has done for you. Keep these forms in a file, so that you can revisit them from time to time and remember all that God has been doing in your life.

Prayer

In your prayer time today, reflect on the importance of faith and righteousness for prayer. Ask the Holy Spirit to closely examine your heart. Are these two things growing in your life? If you're struggling in one of these areas, talk with God about it. Ask for his help to continue growing in your spiritual journey so that your prayers will accomplish much in his kingdom.

James 5:19-20

My brothers, if anyone among you wanders from the truth and someone brings him back, let him know that whoever brings back a sinner from his wandering will save his soul from death and will cover a multitude of sins.

The book of James is a manual for learning how to live a legacy for the glory of God. For the past 30 days we've been learning about the essence of Christian devotion: faith, contentment, perseverance, self-control, obedience, mercy, communication, wisdom, humility, compassion, surrender, generosity, patience, honesty, and prayer. Each of these is important for the success of our personal, spiritual journey. We worship, labor, give, and grow together within the context of the local church.

Yet, as Christian discovered in *A Pilgrim's Progress*, there is much to distract us from our journey of faith. The accounts of people in the Bible who became distracted by the world are many; they include Lot, Samson, Solomon, and Demas. Paul wrote these words about him, "Demas, in love with this present world, has deserted me and gone to Thessalonica (2 Tim 4:10)." That's all we're told, but it's enough. Demas fell victim to one of Satan's biggest traps. Initially, he became distracted by the world. It was hard being a Christian in first-century Rome. As Demas looked around him, he

We can be distracted by this world and lose sight of God's sovereign purpose for our lives.

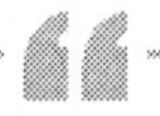

God is the only source of life and blessing; those who depart from him chase only misery and death.

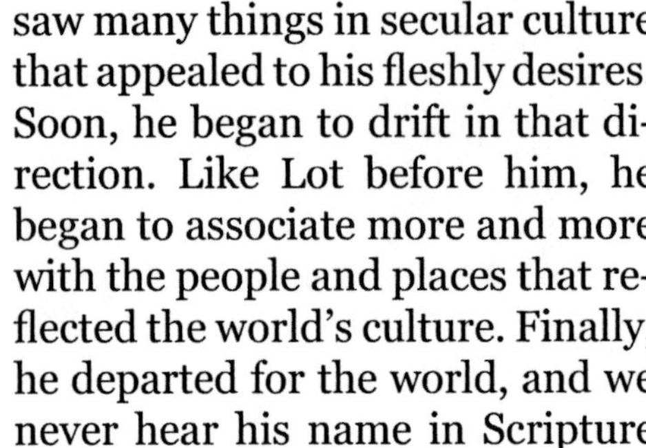

saw many things in secular culture that appealed to his fleshly desires. Soon, he began to drift in that direction. Like Lot before him, he began to associate more and more with the people and places that reflected the world's culture. Finally, he departed for the world, and we never hear his name in Scripture again.

Each of us is capable of making the same choices as Demas. We, too, can be distracted by this world and lose sight of God's sovereign purpose for our lives. James is so concerned about this potential problem that he concludes his book with one final word of admonition—hold one another accountable to Christ so that you will not suffer the tragic consequences of rebellion.

As we begin to look at this text, it is clear that James is writing to Christians. He writes, "If anyone among you wanders from the truth." The phrase "among you" reveals that even those who are members of Christ and his church can become distracted by the world. When this occurs, the things of the world become of greater importance than the things of God. Drifting away from God is the result. The word translated "wanders" means "to stray." Rather than remaining strongly attached to Christ, the gospel, the Scriptures, and the church, the wandering Christian slowly strays away from God. Like a child who loses her way in the woods while chasing after a butterfly, believers who stray away from God often do so gradually—they don't even intend to drift away from God. Yet, as they begin to chase the things that this world offers, they wander further and further away from God and his truth.

Naturally, the further they wander away from God, the less they invest in their spiritual journey. Gradually, they cease to worship, to study the Bible and pray, to serve, to give, or to live in community with other believers. The result is always costly for a Christian. James says that a distracted believer is capable of committing a "multitude of sins," and these sins can ultimately lead to death (1 Tim 6:6-10). The pleasure offered by the world is a mirage, because it promises something that it cannot deliver. God is the only source of life and blessing; those who depart from him chase only misery and death.

God led James to write this book so that we would learn how to develop a legacy of faith. It provides us with the encouragement we need to stay devoted to Christ rather than to drift towards the world. That is why we must begin every day with a renewed commitment to honor Christ with our lives. We must spend time in his word and prayer so that our affections are directed towards Christ and not our own fleshly desires. We must live in authentic community with other Christ-followers within the context of a local church, investing our spiritual gifts and financial resources in God's kingdom.

The importance of living in authentic community with other believers cannot be overstated. In fact, community defined the early church and provided the support necessary to honor Christ in a hostile culture (Acts 2:42-47). But there's another important reason to be engaged in community—we are to hold one another accountable for the state of our spiritual journey.

James ends his book by challenging us to be proactive in this process. He writes, "Let him know that whoever brings back a sinner from his wandering will save his soul from death and will cover a multitude of sins." This verse reveals some important principles. First, every one of us has the potential to wander away from God. The Bible warns us to be humble enough to acknowledge this truth, because understanding our weaknesses will lead us to seek God's strength (Pr 16:18; 2 Cor 12:7-10). God's

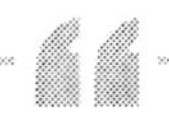

There's another important reason to be engaged in community—we are to hold one another accountable for the state of our spiritual journey.

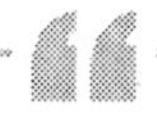

God's strength alone has the power to protect us from the distractions of this world.

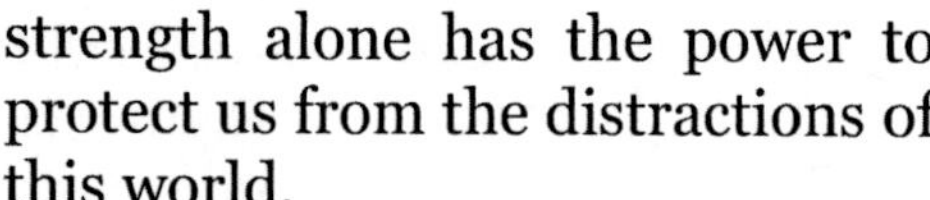

strength alone has the power to protect us from the distractions of this world.

Second, we have a responsibility to help any brother or sister who may be drifting away from God. This is what James means when he talks about bringing back a sinner from his wandering. For this to happen, however, we must be connected with them in community so that we can recognize when this process begins. It generally isn't hard to recognize. When someone we know begins to avoid her participation in a small group, begins to abandon the use of his spiritual gifts, or begins to avoid corporate worship, we know that the "distraction, drift, and depart" process has begun. Rather than ignore it, however, God wants us to lovingly confront him about the choices he is making. The goal is to attempt to protect him from the life-altering or life-destroying choices that sin always produces.

Third, we must approach a distracted brother or sister with the proper motives. The goal isn't to judge them; after all, God is the only judge of our hearts and lives (James 4:12). If we love them, however, we want to spare them from the harsh consequences of sin. Paul gives us some helpful advice at this point. He writes, "If anyone is caught in any transgression, you who are spiritual should restore him in a spirit of gentleness. Keep watch on yourself, lest you too be tempted. Bear one another's burdens, and so fulfill the law of Christ (Gal 6:1-3)." Here, Paul reveals the motive and spirit that should characterize our lives when we attempt to help a distracted brother or sister. Our motive must be love, which reveals itself through a spirit of gentleness. Our spirit must be humble. We must acknowledge that we come not as judges, but as fellow sinners in need of God's grace. The goal is the same for both James and Paul—bear one another's burdens and fulfill the law of Christ (Jn 13:34-35).

Unlike Paul's books, James does not end with any concluding words or salutations. His book simply ends. It appears almost as if he invites us to turn to the beginning and begin again. In this way, the book of James calls us to return over and over again, to reflect on its truth and to embrace its call to live a legacy for the glory of God.

Food for Thought

These final verses may seem curious to you. James has spent his entire book challenging us to walk closely with Christ. Then, at the end, he addresses the challenge of helping those who begin to wander away from God. Why do you think God led him to end with these verses? Think about your own life. Have you ever had a season of spiritual wandering? If so, whom did God use to help draw you back to himself? What are you doing in your life today to protect yourself from becoming distracted by the culture around you?

Faith in Action

Are you currently a part of a small group of believers who share life together within a context of Bible study, prayer, and ministry? If not, consider joining a small group in your church or inviting some people from your church to join you in forming a group. Consider asking each person in your group to get 30 Days to James, or one of the other 30 Days studies, and study a chapter together every week.

Prayer

As you spend time praying today, reflect on all that God has taught you over the past 30 days from the book of James. Ask God to continue to guide you on your journey of faith and to give you opportunities to help other believers on their journey by sharing what you've learned this month. Ask him which 30 Days study to work through next.

Finding L.I.F.E. in Jesus!

Everyone wants to be happy. The hard part is determining exactly what that means. For some, happiness is defined through relationships. They believe that popularity, a huge friend list on Facebook, and a significant other produces happiness. For others, happiness is defined through success. They believe that personal achievement, a huge number in their bank account, and plenty of expensive toys produces happiness. For still others, happiness is defined through community. They believe that personal growth, a huge impact for societal change, and embracing diversity produces happiness. And these things do—until they don't.

Experiencing happiness is as difficult as catching the greased pig at the county fair. It appears to be right in front of us, but then it slips through our fingers and is gone. Friends, achievement, and personal growth have the potential to bring happiness into our lives, but when our friends disappear, success eludes us, and we realize that we're incapable of self-transformation, happiness is quickly replaced by disillusionment and depression. The problem with pursuing happiness is that it is an emotion that is driven by our circumstances. And let's be honest—we all tend to have more negative than positive experiences in our lives.

So, what's the answer? Should we keep doing the same things while expecting different results, or should we consider what Jesus has to say about finding our purpose for life? If you want to stay on the hamster wheel while you try to catch up to happiness, you can stop reading here. But if you're ready to consider what God wants to do in your life, please read on.

God never promises happiness in the Bible. Are you surprised to hear that? Instead, he promises something much greater—joy. While happiness is an emotion fueled by circumstance, joy is an attitude fueled by God's Spirit. Happiness is self-determined. In other words, I am the sole determiner of whether I'm happy at any given moment. Joy, on the other hand, is God-determined. God has promised to give us joy, and it isn't based on our circumstances—it's based on God's character and promises.

This is why Jesus never talks about giving people happiness. He knew all too well that chasing happiness is like chasing your shadow. You can never catch it. Instead, he talks about giving people life. He said, "I came that they may have life and have it abundantly (Jn 10:10)." Here, Jesus reveals that the thing people really want, whether they know it or not, is abundant life. To have an abundant life means that you are personally satisfied in all areas of your life, and you experience peace and contentment as a result. Jesus' statement also means that we do not have the capacity to create that kind of life for ourselves. Jesus came in order to give it to us. But how? The Bible tells us that achieving this kind of satisfied life requires us to know something about God, ourselves, and the reason for the death and resurrection of Jesus Christ.

First, we must understand God's **love**. The Bible says that God is love (I Jn 4:8), and God created us so that we could know him and experience his love (Gen 1:26-31). God created us to be worshipers and to live forever in the reality of his glory. And, when sin marred his perfect creation, he created a plan to free men and women from its curse. At just the right time in history, God sent his own Son, Jesus, into our world. "For God so loved the world, that he gave his only Son, that whoever believes in him should not perish but have eternal life (Jn 3:16)." It is God's love that motivates him to restore relationship with those who are separated from him by sin.

Second, we must understand our **isolation**. To be isolated is to be separated from someone, and as a result, to be alone. This is what sin has done to us. It has separated us from the very one we were created to know, love, and worship—God. When Adam and Eve rebelled against God by breaking the lone command he had given them, the entire world was brought under the curse of sin (Gen 3). As a result, God removed them from the Garden of Eden, and their perfect fellowship with God was broken. In an instant, they had become isolated from God because of their sin. From that moment to this, every person born into this world is guilty of sin. The Bible says, "For all have sinned and fall short of the glory of God (Rom 3:23)." Because of this "there is none righteous, no, not one (Rom 3:10)." Further, "The wages of sin is death (Rom 6:23a)." We were created to love and worship God in perfect community, but now because of sin we are isolated from him. Meanwhile, we try to satisfy this desire to know God by pursuing our own happiness, even though we can never hope to attain it. And in doing so, we risk being isolated from God for all eternity.

Third, we must understand our need for **forgiveness.** There is only one way to experience God's love and escape the isolation caused by sin—we must experience God's forgiveness. In spite of sin, God never stopped loving the people he created. He promised Adam and Eve that he would send someone who could fix the problem they had created. When it was time, God sent his own Son, Jesus, to be the world's Savior. This, too, was an act of God's love. The Bible says, "God shows his love for us in that while we were still sinners, Christ died for us (Rom 5:8)." When Jesus died on the cross, he was paying the penalty for our sins (Rom 3:23-26). When God raised Jesus from the dead, it was to demonstrate that forgiveness was available to all who would receive it by faith.

Paul explains how this happens in his letter to the Ephesians. "For by grace you have been saved through faith. And this is not your own doing; it is the gift of God, not a result of works, so that no one may boast (Eph 2:8-9)."

The reality is that we cannot experience salvation as a result of our own efforts. We can try to be a good person, go to a church, even give a ton of money to worthy causes—none of these "works" can provide forgiveness. No matter how hard we try, we will always "fall short of the glory of God." That is why we must receive God's offer of forgiveness and salvation by faith. Faith simply means to trust or believe. Salvation requires us to believe that God loves us, that we are isolated from him by our sins, and that his Son Jesus died and was raised to life again to pay the sin debt that we owe God because of our sins. When we take God up on his offer of the gift of salvation, he doesn't just give us forgiveness—he gives us life! The Bible says, "The free gift of God is eternal life in Christ Jesus our Lord (Rom 6:23)."

Fourth, we must understand the **enjoyment** that comes from knowing, loving, and worshiping God. Whether we know it or not, we are slaves to sin until God sets us free (Rom 6:20-23). This was the ultimate reason that God sent his Son, Jesus, to die on the cross for our sins—God sent Jesus so that we could be set free from our sins. Jesus said, "You will know the truth, and the truth will set you free. . . . Everyone who commits sin is a slave to sin. . . . So, if the Son sets you free, you will be free indeed (Jn 10:32-36)." Jesus was teaching us that we must be set free from sin in order to enjoy the life that God has given us—both now and in eternity future. We are set free when we commit our lives to Jesus Christ through faith in his death and resurrection. Then, and only then, will we find joy in the abundant life of Jesus Christ!

So, the question for you is a simple one: Are you ready to experience freedom from sin and the abundant life that Jesus promised you? If so, God is waiting for to talk with him about it (Jer 29:13). Stop right where you are and make this your prayer to God,

> "Father in heaven, I know that I'm a sinner. I know that I've done lots of things that displease you and disappoint you. And, I know that I'm isolated from you because of my sin. I know that if I die without knowing you, I will spend forever separated from you in hell. But, I believe that Jesus is your sinless Son, and I believe that he died on the cross for me. I believe that he died to provide a perfect payment for my sin debt. I believe that you raised him from the dead so that I could experience forgiveness for my sins. Right now, Father, I'm asking you to forgive me of my sins and save me. I am receiving your Son Jesus as my personal Lord and Savior. I will follow you the rest of my life. Please give me the joy of a life spent knowing, loving, and worshiping you. I ask these things in Jesus' name, Amen."

If you made the decision to accept Jesus as your Savior today, we want to talk with you! Please contact the people at www.seed-publishing-group.com. We would love to talk with you about your decision and help you with your first steps in following Jesus!